Grammar
in practice 5

40 units of
self-study
grammar
exercises

Roger Gower

with tests

CAMBRIDGE
UNIVERSITY PRESS

CAMBRIDGE UNIVERSITY PRESS
Cambridge, New York, Melbourne, Madrid, Cape Town, Singapore, São Paulo

Cambridge University Press
The Edinburgh Building, Cambridge CB2 2RU, UK

www.cambridge.org
Information on this title: www.cambridge.org/9780521618281

First published 2005

Printed in Italy by Legoprint S.P.A

Typeface Bembo 10.5/12pt. System QuarkXpress® [KAMAE]

A catalogue record for this book is available from the British Library

ISBN -13 978-0-521-61828-1 paperback
ISBN -10 0-521-61828-2

Contents

1 Where do you live?

Question word	auxiliary verb	subject		
	Was(n't)	your assistant	at work yesterday?	No, he wasn't.
	Did(n't)	you	watch TV?	Yes, I did.
	Should(n't)	I	buy some food?	Yes, you should.
Why	**are**	you	learning English?	For my job.
Where	**do**	you	live?	In London.
When	**can**	I	see you?	Tomorrow.
Where	**have**	you	been?	To the bank.
Whose (money)	**is**	it?		It's Sarah's.

Other question words: *Who? What? Which? How many/much/long/far/often/soon?*

ⓘ **Did**n't you go? (Is it true you didn't go?/surprise)

ⓘ 'Who lives there?' 'John does.' NOT ~~Who does live there?~~

A Write the words in the correct order to make questions.

1 you/last night/finish work/did/when   *When did you finish work last night* ?
2 of music/like/Tom/what sort/does ....?
3 get/in the new job/you/will/more money ....?
4 like/countries/you/to visit/would/which ....?
5 last night/meet/who/you/did ....?
6 in New York/live/she/doesn't ....?
7 to your party/came/people/how many ....?
8 car/borrow/did/whose/to get to work/you ....?

B Make questions with a question word and answer them for you.

1 *How long have you been studying* (you/study) English?   *Three years.*
2 _____ (you/usually/do) in the evenings? _____
3 _____ (you/go) on your holidays last year? _____
4 _____ (be) your favourite colour? _____
5 _____ (get up) first in your house? _____
6 _____ (cups of coffee/you/have) this week? _____
7 _____ (you/go out) for dinner? _____
8 _____ (excercise/you/do) each week? _____

C Make questions and match them to the answers.

1 How much/this tour/cost? _*How much does this tour cost?*_ _____F_____
2 Which towns/you/visit on the way? _____
3 Which tour/cost less? _____
4 What/can/see in Oxford? _____
5 Where/the coach/stop? _____
6 Who/live/in the castle? _____
7 children/(not) get/ a reduction? _____
8 Whose/wallet/be/this? _____
9 How soon/the coach/leave? _____

a It's mine.
b Outside your hotel.
c The one to Oxford does.

d In about half an hour.
e Windsor and Reading.
f $90.

g Sorry, no they don't.
h The Queen, for part of the year.
i One of the oldest universities in the world.

2 We meet now and then

Adverb phrases of frequency

I still meet my old schoolfriends **from time to time/every now and again**. (end position)
She goes to yoga classes **twice a week/once in a while**.
From time to time/every now and again I still meet my old schoolfriends.
(front position)
(About) twice a week/Once in a while/Several times a month (frequency + a +
time period) she goes to yoga classes.
Compare: I **never/rarely/hardly ever/sometimes/quite often** take a taxi. (mid position)

Other phrases: *(every) now and then, once every three weeks, most evenings, every five
minutes/evening, every so often* (occasionally), *again and again, at times*

ⓘ Adverb phrases usually go at the end of a sentence. Sometimes they begin a sentence
when the adverb is not the main focus of the sentence.

A **Tim has been asked to write down his signs of stress. Underline
the correct answers.**

STRESS QUESTIONNAIRE - Tim Baker

1 I from time to time/<u>From time to time I</u> find it difficult to sleep.

2 I quite often bite my nails./I bite quite often my nails.

3 I every so often get a headache./I get a headache every so often.

4 I about three times a week work very late./I work very late about
   three times a week.

5 Now and then my mouth feels dry./My mouth now and then feels dry.

6 I several times a day get angry./I get angry several times a day.

7 I am late again and again for appointments./I am late for appointments
   again and again.

B **Write about you. Use an adverb phrase of frequency.**

1 go to bed early ⎯⎯⎯ *I go to bed early from time to time.*

2 do some physical exercise ⎯⎯⎯

3 eat a leisurely meal ⎯⎯⎯

4 have a holiday ⎯⎯⎯

5 sit down and listen to music ⎯⎯⎯

6 have a relaxing warm bath ⎯⎯⎯

3 What are you talking about?

A Complete these sentences with a preposition.

1 'Who are you having lunch *with* tomorrow?'

2 'Look at his picture. Which famous person does he remind you _____?'

3 'I'm going to wait here for another 10 minutes.'
'What *for*?'

4 'I love that coat! Where did you get it *from*?'

5 'Who did you have lunch *with* yesterday?'

6 'This is a great book'.
'What's it *about*?'
'I'm not sure, really. The story is very complicated!'

7 'I've just got a text message.'
'Who _____?'

B Look at the pictures and complete the questions.

1 What _____ *is he thinking about* _____? (he/think)

2 Who _____? (be/the letter)

3 What _____? (she/smile)

4 Who _____? (she/wait)

5 What _____? (she/look)

6 What _____? (she/read)

4 We're having fun

Present simple and continuous / Past simple and continuous

We can use the present or past continuous
- to show an ongoing event or changing situation: My English **was improving** all the time.
- with *always* to emphasise how often something happens: It**'s always raining**. (it's very annoying) She was a happy person. She **was always smiling**. (typical behaviour)

We usually use simple forms with non-action (state) verbs such as *be, feel, have, know, like, prefer, remember, see, think*:
I **think** you're very intelligent. We **had** a good holiday. I **want** some coffee.
However, we can sometimes use some state verbs as action verbs:
You**'re being** very silly at the moment. (for a short period of time)
I**'m seeing** him later. (I have an appointment.)
I**'m thinking** about the future. (considering possibilities)

ⓘ *like* is a state verb: I **like** you. *enjoy* is not a state verb: I **enjoy** parties. (in general) I**'m enjoying** this party. (now)

ⓘ Some verbs can be used as state verbs or action verbs: We **have** a good life. (state verb = possess) He**'s having** dinner/a rest. (action verb)

A Complete the sentences with *always* + the verbs in the box in the present continuous.

> argue   complain   give   go off   lose   ~~run out~~

1    2    3

4    5    6

1 The coffee *'s always running out* .
2 They're friends but they ....
3 The fire alarm ....
4 He .... his keys.
5 She's so nice. She .... presents to people.
6 He's very fussy. He .... about the food.

B Underline the correct answer.

Conference Centre

1 'I <u>see</u>/'m seeing you're staying here in the conference centre.'
  'Yes, I <u>prefer</u>/'m preferring it to staying in a hotel.'
2 'What **do you think/are you thinking** of the presentations?'
  'I **enjoy/'m enjoying** them a lot.'
3 'This conference **becomes/is becoming** much more popular.'
  'Yes, I **remember/'m remembering** a few years ago there was almost
  no-one here.'
4 '**Do you like/Are you liking** working in this country?'
  'No, I **think/'m thinking** of moving to Brazil.'
5 'Good jobs **get/are getting** much harder to find in Brazil these days.'
  'I **know/'m knowing**. My work colleagues **always tell/are always telling** me
  to stay where I am.'

C Complete the email with a verb from the box in the correct form.
  Use the present simple and continuous and the past simple and
  continuous.

Denmark

---

be not/feel always/get on only/go up have improve
like see start think

Denmark's not a big country – although there (1) .... *are* .... more
than 500 islands – and the population of just over 5 million (2)
.... by less than 0.5% each year. I (3) ....
it is lovely place to live. In general people (4) .... a good
standard of living, and health-care is excellent, although unemployment
(5) .... to increase (it's about 6% at the moment).

As I (6) .... cycling, and the country is so flat, in the
summer holidays I (7) .... my bike to explore some lovely
fishing village somewhere.

My Danish (8) .... slowly but I (9) ....
confident yet. I (10) .... my Danish teacher this afternoon to
arrange extra classes.

5 While I was sleeping

for/during/while; by/until

for + period of time (It answers the question *How long...?*)

I lived in China **for** two years. NOT ~~during two years~~

during + noun (It answers the question *When...?*)

I met her **during** the summer. (at some point in the summer)
The hotels are full **during** the summer. (all through the summer)

while + subject + verb (It answers the question *When...?*)

I met her **while** I was living in London. (at the same time as)

by + a point in time

They should be here **by** now. (before now)

until + a point in time

I'll be at work **until** six. (continue working then stop at six)

A Write the correct word in the gap.

1 Please wait there _____until_____ we call you. (until/by)

2 Have a coffee _____ you're waiting. (during/while)

3 Read a magazine _____ a few minutes. (during/for)

4 At some time _____ the examination, the nurse will take a blood sample. (during/for)

5 Have you taken any aspirin _____ the last week? (while/during)

6 You'll be finished _____ five o'clock. (until/by)

B A patient is talking to a doctor. Complete the conversation with *for, during, while, by* or *until*.

I've had a bad back (1) __*for*__ years but it got a lot worse (2) _____ the morning yesterday (3) _____ I was out shopping. I had to sit down, and couldn't move (4) _____ my husband arrived in the car. (5) _____ the time we got home I was in agony!

Don't go back to work (6) _____ you feel better, and (7) _____ you are recovering, get plenty of rest. You can take pain killers (8) _____ the next day or two but then stop. With a bit of luck, you should be able to move normally (9) _____ the end of next week. If so, you can go back to work, but (10) _____ you're there don't try and lift anything heavy!

6 I used to live alone

A Read this extract from a book about
childhood memories. Where possible,
change the words in italics to *would* + verb.
If not possible, write X.

Family holidays are my happiest memories of childhood.
My father *used to be* (1) .... X .... a GP and ran his
practice in our family home so we *used to share*
(2) *would share* the house with around 200
strangers every week. Also, the telephone *never used to stop*
(3) .... ringing. It was good to get away.
We *used to leave* (4) .... before dawn and get
ahead of the traffic. I remember we *used to have* (5) .... a dog called
Ross, who came with us. We *usually went* (6) .... to Scotland and I *used
to like* (7) .... walking on the sandy beaches. On wet days
we *used to play* (8) .... cards and read novels.
When I *swam* (9) .... in the Mediterranean for the first
time I *was* (10) .... surprised how warm it was!

B Underline the correct alternative. Then complete these sentences
about yourself.

1 I **used to**/would have a close relationship *with my brother when I was younger*.

2 I **used to/would** live ...., but now I
....

3 .... **didn't use to/wouldn't** be
.... but .... now.

4 I don't like .... now but I **would/used to** when
....

5 When I was at college I **would/used to** often ....

7 The whole day

A Write the correct word in the gap.

> **COLLEGE HANDBOOK**
>
> 1 ___*All*___ mobile phones should be switched off during lectures. (all/every)
>
> 2 _____ student taking part in sporting activities must wear appropriate games kit. (all/every)
>
> 3 _____ personal property should be clearly marked with your name. (all/each)
>
> 4 If you lose a book which is part of a set, you might be asked to replace _____ set. (every/the whole)
>
> 5 _____ day of sickness must be reported to your personal tutor. (each/all)
>
> 6 _____ student is expected to help keep the college tidy. (all the/every)
>
> 7 You are expected to be on time for _____ lectures. (all of your/every)

B Complete the gaps with *all, whole, each, every*.

1 Nearly ___*all*___ the students live near the college.

2 There are two libraries. In _____ you will find an outstanding selection of teaching materials.

3 The _____ college is closed during public holidays.

4 Not _____ students can afford to have their own laptop.

5 There is a _____ day of staff training before college begins.

6 Nearly _____ member of staff has worked here for several years.

8 After talking to you

After (+ past simple/-*ing*)			
	First action		Second action
After	**she phoned phoning**	her brother,	she went out.

Before (+ past simple/-*ing*)			
	Second action		First action
Before	**I went going**	to bed,	I watched TV.

ⓘ We can also say:
She went out a few minutes **after she phoned/phoning** her brother.
I watched TV **before I went/going** to bed.

A Complete the sentences with the correct form of the verb.

1 After .... *leaving* .... university, I had to find a job. (leave)

2 Before I .... for an interview, I bought a new suit. (go)

3 I applied for a job in a museum after .... an advert in the paper. (see)

4 Before .... work, I had to sell my apartment in London. (start)

5 After .... somewhere to live, I decided to buy a car. (find)

6 I had to pass my driving test before I .... drive the car. (can)

B Join the two sentences using the word(s) in brackets. Use the past simple or -*ing*. (1 = first action; 2 = second action)

1 The 5-year old Pu-Yi ruled China.(1) He gave up his position as Emperor in 1912.(2) (Before)
Before he gave up his position as Emperor in 1912, the 5 year old Pu-Yi ruled China.
Before giving up his position as Emperor in 1912, the 5 year old Pu-Yi ruled China.

2 Joan of Arc worked on her father's farm.(1) She led a French army against the British.(2) (Before)

....

3 Mikhail Gorbachev agreed an arms treaty with the US.(1) He was awarded the Nobel Peace Prize.(2) (Three years after)

....

4 She asked to be buried with the Roman Marc Antony.(1) Cleopatra ended her life.(2) (Before)

....

9 He's quite nice

Adverbs of degree: *really/very; rather/fairly; a bit; quite*

To make adjectives/adverbs stronger: *really/very (a really/a very)*
It was **very/really** good. It was a **very/really** good film.

To make adjectives or adverbs weaker: *rather, fairly, quite*
He walks **rather/fairly/quite** slowly.

ⓘ We usually use *rather* for ideas we think are negative: The film was **rather** boring.

ⓘ He's **a rather/a fairly** shy person. He's **rather a/quite a** shy person. NOT ~~He's a quite shy person.~~ NOT ~~He's fairly a shy person.~~

ⓘ We can sometimes use:
• *quite* before extreme adjectives like *exhausted, brilliant, amazing* or absolute adjectives like *true, wrong* to mean 'completely'. I was **quite exhausted**. He was **quite wrong**.
• *a bit* (= a little) with negative adjectives. I'm **a bit tired**. NOT ~~He's a bit tired person.~~ NOT ~~He's a bit nice.~~

A Complete the sentences with the correct adverb.

1 Buses run _____quite_____ frequently from here to the city centre. (a bit/quite)

2 The Forbidden City is _____ magnificent. You must go there. (quite/fairly)

3 It's _____ far to walk to the Summer Palace. I suggest you take a taxi. (a bit/a fairly)

4 The China World is _____ expensive hotel. This hotel is much cheaper. (fairly an/rather an)

5 The Zhu Bao Silk Market is _____ small market and not very touristy. (a quite/quite a)

6 It's _____ cold day outside. You'll need a coat. (a rather/a bit)

B Complete the sentences with a word from the box and the word in brackets. Use *a/an* if necessary.

| cheap busy interesting old ~~beautiful~~ |

1 On 1st May Beijing is *very beautiful* – the city is decorated with flowers. (very)

2 You won't need much money. Taxis are _____ . (fairly)

3 Sunday is a day off for most people and all the parks get _____ . (rather)

4 The Quanjude is _____ Peking Duck restaurant. It was opened in 1864. (really)

5 It was _____ guidebook – it had a lot of useful information. (quite)

10 They had already left

Past perfect

Positive			Negative		
I/He/She You/We/They	**had** (**'d**)	arriv**ed**.	I/He/She You/We/They	**hadn't**	arriv**ed**.

Questions			Short answers		
Had	I/he/she/it we/you/they	**left**?	Yes,	I/he/she/it we/you/they	**had**.
			No,	I/he/she/it we/you/they	**hadn't**

ⓘ We use the past perfect to talk about events/actions before a past time.
When/By the time we got to the airport, the plane **had** already **left**.

```
          plane left    got to airport    now
PAST ————————— X ——————————— X —————————— | ————————►
```

However, if the order of events is clear we often prefer the past simple.
The plane **left** before we **got** to the airport.

ⓘ We use *already*, *yet*, *ever/never* to emphasise the event which happened first.
The plane had **already** left. Had they **ever** met? I had **never** been there.

A Write the past perfect of these verbs in the positive (+) or negative (–).

1 (forget +) _had forgotten_   2 (go –) _hadn't been/gone_   3 (see +) ....

4 (pay +) ....   5 (hear –) ....   6 (have +) ....

7 (have –) ....   8 (start +) ....   9 (book –) ....

B Match the two halves of the sentences.

1 When I'd paid for the tickets   *h*   a so we were glad we went.

2 We didn't want anything to eat   ....   b because I hadn't booked good seats.

3 One man had forgotten his ticket   ....   c but the show had already started.

4 The concert was sold out   ....   d because we'd had a big pizza.

5 We hadn't heard her live before   ....   e so I nearly fell asleep.

6 We eventually found our seats   ....   f because the singer had been on TV a lot.

7 We couldn't see very well   ....   g and they wouldn't let him in.

8 I hadn't been to bed for ages   ....   h we joined the queue to get in.

C Complete the sentences about Nina Simone (born Eunice Wayman 1933). Use the past perfect in the positive or negative and add *already* in Questions 1–6.

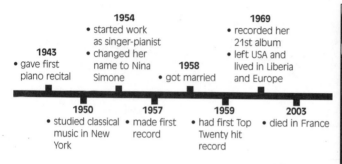

1 By the time she arrived in New York, she _had already given_ piano recitals.

2 When she started work as a singer–pianist, she _____ classical music in New York.

3 By 1955, she _____ work as a singer–pianist.

4 By the time she made her first record, she _____ her name to Nina Simone.

5 By the time she got married, she _____ her first record.

6 By 1960, she _____ her first Top Twenty hit record.

7 When she left America, she _____ 21 albums.

8 By the time she died, she _____ in America for 34 years.

D Complete this interview between a journalist and a friend of Nina Simone's.

1 'When she started work _had she ever studied_ (ever/study) music?'
   ' _Yes, she had_ .'

2 'When she gave her first recital, _____ (already/change) her name?'
   ' _____ .'

3 ' _____ (already/make) her first record by the time she got married?'
   ' _____ ,'

4 ' _____ (have) a Top Twenty hit by 1958?'
   ' _____ ,'

5 'How many albums _____ (record) by the time she left America?'
   ' _____ ,'

6 'How many years _____ (live) abroad by the time she died?'
   ' _____ ,'

Test 1 (Units 1–10)

A Circle the correct form.

1 How long **the meeting will/will the meeting** last?
2 She **every few minutes phones her friends/phones her friends every few minutes**.
3 Who **with did you go out last night/did you go out with last night?**
4 I hate my car – it **always breaks/is always breaking** down!
5 I'll wait **by/until** you're ready.
6 He **used to be/would be** very thin.
7 Nearly **every/all** apartment is occupied.
8 After **playing/play** tennis I have a shower.
9 It's a **fairly/bit** good film.
10 By the time I arrived, the shops **closed/had closed**.

10

B Write questions. The words underlined are the answers.

1 She works <u>in a bank</u>. _____
2 I got the book <u>from the library</u>. _____
3 <u>Yes</u>, I should be more careful. _____
4 <u>Tom</u> invited me to the party. _____
5 The plane leaves <u>from Kennedy Airport</u>. _____
6 <u>Yes</u>, I had already paid for the tickets. _____
7 <u>My</u> car was stolen last night. _____
8 The book was <u>about a young politician</u>. _____
9 We've been living here <u>for six months</u>. _____
10 <u>Sarah</u> told me the news. _____

10

C Write the words in the correct order.

1 visit/my father/I/most afternoons _____
2 reads/a newspaper/rarely/she _____
3 all/we/from time to time/get lost _____
4 hardly ever/for himself/cooks/he _____
5 work late/have to/we/twice a week _____

5

D Write the verbs in the correct form.

1 I (have) .... dinner when you phoned last night.

2 We (already/ leave) .... by the time Brian arrived.

3 He's so bad-tempered. He (always/get) .... angry with people.

4 I (think) .... about the problem right now.

5 I (usually/prefer) .... coffee to tea.

6 Before (go) .... to bed, I always read a book.

7 I (never/be) .... to Peru before last year.

8 '(you/enjoy) .... the meal?' 'Yes, it's delicious.'

9 At the moment the traffic (get) .... worse.

10 Before I (go) .... out, I phoned my daughter. **10**

E Rewrite the sentences with the expression in brackets.

1 Every night I went for a run. (would) ....

2 We had two beautiful cats. (used to) ....

3 Did you live in Argentina? (used to) ....

4 They met every Sunday. (would) ....

5 I didn't have a computer. (used to) **5**

F Complete the gaps with the correct word.

1 .... of my friends live in Mexico. (all/every)

2 It's .... a cold day. (fairly/quite)

3 We stayed there the .... evening. (whole/all)

4 .... of the two bedrooms has a bathroom. (every/each)

5 That's .... a strange thing to say! (very/rather) **5**

G Correct the mistakes.

1 'Who <u>did ring</u> you?' 'John did.' ....

2 I worked in the bank <u>during</u> two years. ....

3 There is still <u>all a month</u> before my birthday. ....

4 There is <u>a quite a lot</u> of food in the fridge. ....

5 Your parents should have got here <u>until</u> now. **5**

TOTAL

50

18

11 He left 10 minutes ago

Present perfect or past simple? ▶▶ Verb forms page 65

We use the past simple to talk about actions that began and finished in the past:
I **met** her yesterday. I **worked** in a bank when I was younger.

We use the present perfect to talk about actions/situations that:
• began and finished in the (recent) past but affect the present.
Look! The aircraft**'s** (just) **landed**. They'll be with us soon.
• continue from the past until now.
I've been a teacher all my life.
I've seen him today. (It is still today) I **saw** him this morning. (It is now afternoon/evening.)

ⓘ We usually use a definite time expression (*last night, two weeks ago*) with the past simple to talk about completed actions at a specific time in the past.

ⓘ We use *yet/still/already* + present perfect to talk about things that have happened (or not happened) up to now. Have you read the book **yet**? He **still** hasn't rung me. She's **already** seen the film.
We use *How long?/for/since* + present perfect/present perfect continuous to talk about situations/actions that started in the past and are continuing now. I've worked/been working here **for** 10 years.

A Write the verbs in the past simple or present perfect.

1 I like Hákan. I first ___*met*___ (meet) him at
university and we *'ve remained* (remain)
friends ever since.

2 Where is Agnes now? I _____ (not/see)
her for ages. We _____ (go) out together once after we first _____
(meet) but the evening _____ (not/be) a great success.

3 Apparently, Tomas _____ (leave) home at half-past-six but he
_____ (still/not/arrive). Do you know where he is?

4 Monika _____ (play) clarinet for the local orchestra for about two years
now. She _____ (first/take up) the instrument when her sister
_____ (buy) her one for her birthday.

5 It's late. I'm going home to bed. By the way, _____ (you/speak) to Jan
this morning?

6 Hurry up! The concert _____ (already/start). _____
(you/not/get) a taxi yet?

B Write about you. Use the past simple or present perfect.

1 I have always _____   4 I _____ last year.

2 I first _____   5 I _____ this month.

3 I've often _____

12 You'd better sit down

should/ought to/had better/If I were you...

You	should ought to 'd (had) better	leave.	**Should** we leave?	Yes, you **should**. No, you **shouldn't**.
You	shouldn't 'd better not	stay in.	**If I were you, I'd** leave now. **I'd** leave now **if I were you**.	

You **should** (definitely) read it – it's a great book. (recommendation)
You (certainly) **shouldn't** go to work today – you really don't look well. (advice)
It's cold. You'**d** (really) **better** wear a coat. (It's a good thing to do now – stronger than *should/ought to. Had better* refers to the present or the future, not the past.)

ⓘ *Should, ought to, had better* are modals. He **should/ought** to NOT ~~He shoulds/oughts to~~

ⓘ *Should* is more common than *ought to.* We do not usually use: *ought to* in negatives; *ought to/had better* in questions.

A This woman's son is having problems sleeping. Rewrite the sentences, using the word in brackets in the positive or negative.

1 It's a good idea for your son to get more regular exercise. (should)
   Your son should get _____ more regular exercise.

2 It's not a good idea for him to eat a large meal before bedtime. (should)
   _____ a large meal before bedtime.

3 It might be a good idea to buy him a different mattress. (if)
   _____ a different mattress.

4 I don't think he should watch so much TV in the evenings. (better)
   _____ so much TV in the evenings.

5 It's a good idea for him to go to bed earlier. (ought)
   _____ to bed earlier.

B Complete this email with the words in the box in the positive or negative and any other words you need.

| better/carry better/climb ~~get~~ leave ought/wear should/go |

If (1) ___ *I were you, I'd get* ___ a weather forecast first – conditions can
change very quickly. You definitely (2) _____ if it's
stormy. Also, you (3) _____ proper walking boots –
your feet will get very sore otherwise. It's very easy to get lost, so you
(4) _____ a whistle, and if (5) _____
the details of your planned route with a friend. As it's your first walk in these
hills, you (6) _____ too high. It could be very risky.

13 Do you think you could ...?

Requests

Will you/Would you/Can you (informal)	
Could you please Do you think you could I wonder/was wondering if you could I don't suppose you could Would it be possible for you to	**carry** my suitcase for me?
Do/Would you mind I wonder/I was wondering if you'd mind	**carrying** my suitcase for me?

ⓘ We add *not* for the negative: Would you **not** touch/Would you mind **not** touching that vase?

ⓘ We add *possibly* to make an expression more polite: Do you think you could **possibly**...?

ⓘ 'Do you mind.../Would you mind....?' 'Of course not.'/'Not at all.' (= yes)

ⓘ When we cannot say *'yes'* to a request we usually apologise and give a reason: 'Can you make some coffee?' 'I'm sorry, I can't. I've got to go.'

A Write the verb in the correct form.

1 'I don't suppose you ___*could help*___ (help) me with my luggage, ___*could*___ you?' 'No problem.'

2 'Would it be possible for you _____ (turn) down your music a little? I'm trying to work.' 'Sure.'

3 'Would you mind _____ (not/put) your feet on the seat? People have to sit there.' 'OK.'

4 'Do you think you _____ (possibly/shut) this window for me? It seems to be stuck.' 'Of course.'

5 'I was wondering if you _____ (mind/look after) my suitcase for a few minutes?' 'No, of course not.'

B Make these requests more polite.

1 'Fill in this form.' 'Would you mind ___*filling in this form*___ ?'

2 'Do me a favour.' 'I wonder _____ ?'

3 'Don't make so much noise!' 'Do you think _____ ?'

4 'Give me a lift into town.' 'Could you please _____ ?'

5 'Lend me some money.' 'I don't suppose _____ ?'

6 'Don't drop litter in the street!' 'Would you mind _____ ?'

14 I'll do it before I leave

before/after/as soon as/while

Main clause		Future time clause (verb in the present)
Close the window	**before**	you go out.
We'll talk about it	**after**	I get back.
Let me know	**as soon as**	you hear any news.
You can borrow my car	**while**	I'm in Scotland.

ⓘ We usually use a comma if the time clause comes first:
Before you leave, come and see me.

A Complete the sentences with *before*, *after*, *as soon as* or *while*.

1 I'll have a word with the manager __*before*__ I decide what to do.

2 I really want to know if you passed your exam. Give me a ring .... you get the results.

3 Can you hold this .... I put the rubbish outside?

4 I'll look for a job soon .... I graduate.

5 Get to the exhibition at least two hours .... it closes or you won't see very much.

6 Would you give her the message .... she phones?

B Correct the mistakes in the messages.

1
Can you cook dinner
before we will get
home?
Can you cook
dinner before
we get home?

2
As soon as the
post is arriving
can you give me
a ring?
....
....

3
Don't use my computer
while I'm being out!
....
....
....

4
Tell the kids to go to
bed as soon as the
film finish.
....
....
....

5
Don't forget to clean
up the flat after
your friends will leave.
....
....
....

6
Can you wash the dishes
before you are going to
work in the morning?
....
....
....

15 I made it myself

Reflexive pronouns; *own*; *each other/one another*

We use reflexives pronouns:
- when the object of the verb is the same as the subject. He made **himself** an omelette. (he made an omelette for himself)
- with some verbs when there is no direct object. behave/enjoy **yourself**; hurt **themselves**
- to stress a noun. The job **itself** wasn't difficult, but I had to work long hours.
- with *by* to mean 'alone'. She went to the cinema **by herself**.

We use *own* to mean: 'without help' (He cuts his **own** hair.) 'alone' (She went **on** her **own**.) 'belonging to no other person' (This is my **own** room.)

We use *each other/one another* when one or more person does something to or for the other person(s). They talked to **each other/one another**. They wrote down **each other's/one another's** address.

A Underline the correct answer to complete the college rules.

1 We live as a community – don't just think about <u>yourself</u>/**your own**/**each other**.

2 Help **you**/**one another**/**your own** at all times.

COMMUNITY
RESIDENTIAL
COLLEGE

3 Don't walk around the grounds **yourself**/**yourselves**/**on your own** at nights.

4 We don't have cleaners – you will need to do **yourselves**/**your own**/**by yourself** cleaning.

5 You will all need photos of **yourself**/**yourselves**/**one another**/**each other** for your ID cards.

6 The residence is open at the weekends but the college **by itself**/**on its own**/**itself** is closed.

7 Students must not be in **each other**/**each other's**/**one another** rooms after midnight.

B Complete the sentences.

1 I've bought a book and I'm teaching _*myself*_ to play the guitar.

2 Some students are very dependent – they don't do anything by ....

3 I don't like being on .... – I much prefer it when we're all together.

4 Sometimes my friends meet in the Common Room and we help .... with our projects.

5 There aren't any cleaners. We have to do all the cleaning ....

6 I'm really enjoying .... – the course is great, and the people are very kind.

16 She put on a coat to keep warm

Clauses of purpose: *in order that/so that; in order to/so as to/to; in case*

We use clauses of purpose to answer the question *What for?* or *Why?*

		+ infinitive
We go to work	to **in order to** **so as to**	earn money.
		+ subject + verb
I'll give you his address	**so (that)**	you can call in and see him.
		+ present tense (for the future)/ past tense (for the past)
Take your mobile phone	**in case**	I need to speak to you. (it's possible I might)
		+ noun/-*ing*
I'm saving	**for**	a new car.
This machine is		cutting glass. (saying what a *thing* is for)

ⓘI hurried **so as not to** miss the bus. I hurried **in order not to** miss the bus. I hurried **so (that)** I wouldn't miss the bus. NOT ~~I hurried not to miss the bus.~~

ⓘNOT ~~I'm saving for buying/for to buy a new car.~~

ⓘNOT ~~Take your mobile phone if I need to speak to you.~~

A Underline the correct answers in these extracts from a biography about the TV natural historian, Sir David Attenborough.

1 Sir David Attenborough travels round the world **to/so that** film wild life programmes for TV.

2 He takes classical music CDs with him **in case/so that** he gets bored on flights.

3 The film crew spend many months preparing **in order to/for** make sure they get good pictures.

4 They use special equipment **for/in order to** filming at night.

5 He works with the world's best scientists **so that/so as to** he understands as much as possible about his subjects.

6 He whispers when filming **so as not to/not to** disturb the animals and **to/for** make us feel we are really there.

B Complete the sentences.

1 Sir David Attenborough uses a personal style of story telling _____*to*_____ help us see into the animals' secret lives.

2 He wants to make us love wildlife _____so that_____ we will then learn to protect it.

3 In one programme he went into the water in _____order to_____ listen to whale songs for himself.

4 He doesn't like going into dark caves _____ there are rats there – they are the only animals he hates!

5 He travelled 260,000 miles _____ his programme on birds.

C Complete these extracts from an environmental website. In some cases there is more than one answer.

Earthwatch

1 Join us _____*to help*_____ (help) protect the environment.

2 We need to act urgently so _____ (stop) climate change.

3 Write to your government in _____ (complain) about its environmental policy.

4 We should stop using CFC sprays _____ (we/damage) the ozone layer even more.

5 We sometimes use non-violent protest _____ (achieve) our aims.

6 Campaign against whaling _____ (we/protect) the whales.

7 We have our own ships for _____ (find out) what's going on at sea.

D Complete these sentences. Use *to, so as (not) to, so that, for, in order to, in case.*

1 What are you studying English for?
   In order to get a good job when I leave college.

2 Why do people make lists before they go shopping?

3 Do you exercise regularly? What for?

4 Why do some people take travellers cheques when they travel abroad?

5 Have you got a laptop computer? What for?

6 Why shouldn't we drink too much coffee in a day?

17 I'd rather stay in

prefer + noun/-ing	
I (much) **prefer**	tea **to** coffee (noun)/swimming **to** jogging (*-ing*). **to sleep/sleeping** late than **to get up/getting up** early. (in general)
*'d prefer + to-*infinitive	
I'd **prefer**	**to go** out (rather) **than** (to) stay at home. Come on, let's go. **not to go** out. Let's stay at home. (particular situation)

'd rather/'d sooner	+ bare infinitive
I'd (much/far) **rather/I'd sooner**	**(not) go** by car. (particular situation)

('d) prefer you to... /('d) prefer it if you... I'd rather you... I'd sooner you...

I'd **prefer you** to cook./I'd **prefer it if you cooked/didn't cook**. (now or in the future)
I'd **rather/'d sooner you cooked (didn't cook)**. (now or in the future)
I'd **rather/sooner he'd (hadn't) come**. (in the past)

A Two hotel guests are talking in their rooms.

1 I'd rather not ___*c*___   **a** if we went into town tonight.

2 I'd sooner you ___   **b** New York hotels to London hotels.

3 I much prefer ___   **c** eat in the dining room. Let's ask for room service.

4 I'd prefer it ___   **d** we had booked somewhere quieter. This is too noisy.

5 I'd rather ___   **e** went down to complain rather than me.

B Write answers using the word in brackets.

1 'Let's watch TV.' 'No, I'd rather ___*go to the cinema.*___ '

2 'Do you want to be a teacher?' 'No, I'd prefer ___ .'

3 'Can I borrow your bike?' 'No, I'd prefer it ___ .'

4 'Would you like an aspirin?' 'No, I'd rather not ___ pills.'

5 'Let's play tennis?' 'No, I'd sooner we ___ .'

6 'Did you like New York?' 'No, I'd rather we ___ .'

18 Try phoning her at home

A Underline the correct answer.

1 a I remember **getting/to get** the
   tickets but I can't find them anywhere.

   b I must remember **watching/to watch**
   that DVD. Perhaps I will this evening.

2 a Don't forget **meeting/to meet** me outside at 6 o'clock. OK?

   b I'll never forget **seeing/to see** my first James Bond film. It was great.

3 a I tried **buying/to buy** my favourite early Chaplin film but I couldn't find a
   copy anywhere.

   b Have you tried **looking/to look** on the internet? You might find someone
   has a copy for sale.

4 a My local cinema has stopped **showing/to show** foreign films. It's a pity
   because I like them.

   b Let's stop **having/to have** a cup of coffee before we go to the cinema.

5 a The young couple went on **talking/to talk** after the film had started.

   b After leaving the cinema we went on **meeting/to meet** our friends for dinner.

6 a The film starts at 7 o'clock. That means **leaving/to leave** now. I want to get
   there on time!

   b Sorry I didn't tell you about the film. I meant **phoning/to phone** you last
   night but I forgot.

7 a I saw him **parking/park** the car and cross the road.

   b We listened to them **playing/to play** outside the cinema.

B Complete the sentences.

1 As I walked in, one of the characters in the film was chasing Harry Potter.

As I walked in, I saw one of the characters in the film __*chasing*__ Harry Potter.

2 Something quickly touched my arm in the dark.

I felt something quickly .... my arm in the dark.

3 The person next to me dropped something on the floor.

I heard the person next to me .... something on the floor.

4 Tania thought something was burning.

Tania thought she could smell something ....

5 As we left the cinema a lot of people were queuing to get in.

As we left the cinema we saw a lot people .... to get in.

C Write the verbs in the correct form in this film review.

The James Bond adventure *Die Another Day* tells the story of billionaire Gustav Graves, who plans (1) __*to destroy*__ (destroy) the world. At the beginning of the film we see James Bond (2) .... (suffer) in prison but he is allowed (3) .... (go) free after his boss in London manages (4) .... (exchange) him for other prisoners. The film is very fast and keeps on (5) .... (move) between different locations (Cuba, London, Iceland and North Korea) as Bond, and American agent Jinx, played by Halle Berry, try (6) .... (stop) the evil Graves.

D Complete these sentences for you. Use a verb.

1 I'll never forget ....

2 Some films make me ....

3 I regret not ....

4 I always meant ....

5 I prefer ....

6 Last night I saw someone ....

7 I've never tried ....

19 I had been working all day

Past perfect continuous

Positive			Negative		
I/He/She /It You/We/They	**had been** play**ing**.		I/He/She/It You/We/They	**hadn't (had not) been** play**ing**.	
Questions			Short answers		
Had	I/he/she it/we/ you/they	**been** play**ing**?	No,	I/he/she it/we you/they	**hadn't**
			Yes,	I/he/she it/we you/they	**had.**

We use the past perfect continuous to talk about a temporary activity in progress over a period of time up to a specific time in the past.
Before I went to Rome (specific time in the past), I **had been living** in Moscow for 3 years (earlier temporary activity).

ⓘ The past perfect continuous focuses on the activity, not the completed event.

A Write the verbs in the past perfect continuous.

1 Before you got here, (I/talk) *I had been talking* to my sister for about an hour.

2 (It/rain) _____ all morning so we decided to cancel our picnic.

3 My eyes were red when you got here because (I/cry) _____ .

4 '_____ (you/wait) for long when she got there?'
'No, we _____ ?'

5 I sounded strange when you called because (I/sleep) _____ .

B Write the verbs in the past perfect or the past perfect continuous.

When the police stopped me I
(1) *had been driving* (drive) over the
speed limit for several kilometres. The
reason was that a couple of hours before
that, the hospital (2) _____
(phone) to say that my wife was going to
have a baby later that evening. I was very
tired because I (3) _____ (work) hard all day. As I (4)
_____ (look forward to) this moment for so long, I didn't realise how
fast I was driving. Luckily, the police were sympathetic. I told them I (5)
_____ (only/try) to get to the hospital to be with my wife, and they
gave me a warning. Unfortunately, though, I (6) _____ (forget) the
way to the hospital and by the time I got there our baby (7) _____
(already/be) born.

20 We needn't have hurried

need (to)

I **need to** do some shopping. You **need to** see a doctor. (I think it's necessary.)
You **don't need to/needn't** wash those dishes. They're clean. (I think it's not necessary.)

ⓘ Question: *Does he need to...?* or *Need he...?*

ⓘ Compare: You **needn't** send me an email. (It's not necessary.) You **mustn't** send me an email. (Don't send me an email! It's the wrong thing to do.)

didn't need to/needn't have

There were plenty of seats of the train. We **didn't need to** stand. (It wasn't necessary.)
There were plenty of seats of the train. We **needn't have** stood. (It wasn't necessary but we did stand.)

A Complete the sentences with the words in the box and *need(n't)*.

| ask | be | ~~do~~ | eat | organize | wear |

1 You *don't need to do* an IT training course for this job, but it helps.

2 You _____ in the office by 8.55 am. We start work promptly at 9.00.

3 You _____ your time carefully. It's easy to spend the day doing nothing.

4 You _____ a suit on Fridays. We're allowed to be casual.

5 If you want a locker, you _____ the personnel manager.

6 You _____ in the canteen. There's a very good restaurant next door.

B Rewrite the sentences with *didn't need to* or *needn't have*.

1 I arrived early for the interview but it wasn't necessary.
I _*needn't have arrived early*_ for the interview.

2 It wasn't necessary to spend the whole afternoon with the company so I didn't.
I _____ the whole afternoon with the company.

3 I was worried, but it wasn't necessary. The interviewers were very friendly.
I _____ . The interviewers were very friendly.

4 They said it wasn't necessary to take any certificates, so I left them at home.
They said I _____ any certificates, so I left them at home.

5 I gave them the names of three referees but they only wanted two.
I _____ the names of three referees. They only wanted two.

Test 2 (Units 11–20)

A Circle the correct form.

1 I still **didn't see/haven't seen** that film. Is it still showing?

2 You **ought to go/ought go** to bed early tonight.

3 Do you think you **possibly give/could possibly give** me a hand?

4 I'll come as soon as I **finish/will finish** work.

5 She went on holiday **by herself/her own**.

6 Take an umbrella **so that/in case** it rains.

7 I'd prefer **you phone/it if you phoned** when you arrive tomorrow.

8 Sorry! I didn't mean **interrupt/to interrupt/interrupting** you.

9 I was very tired because I**'ve been working/'d been working** hard all day.

10 I **needn't have caught/didn't need to catch** the bus because
Tom gave me a lift.

10

B Write the verbs in the correct form.

1 I _____ (go) Scotland 5 years ago but I _____ (not/go)
there since.

2 'How long _____ (you/decorate) your house now?' 'For about
two months.'

3 If I _____ (be) you, I _____ (look for) a new job.

4 Before you _____ (leave) London next week, you _____
(should/go) to a show.

5 I'd prefer _____ (eat) at home tonight than _____ (go) out
to a restaurant.

6 I remember _____ (lend) you 20 dollars. Can you give it back?

7 I wish I could stop _____ (sneeze)!

8 I _____ (work) in Tokyo for six months when I decided I needed
a holiday.

9 After the guests went home, I was very pleased I _____ (cook) a
meal for so many people.

10 No, you _____ (not/need) to pay for these drinks. Take one –
they're free!

10

C Complete the gaps with one word.

1 'Do you mind closing the door?' '............... at all.'

2 Look after yourself .... we're away on holiday!

3 Remind me to give you my address .... you leave, or I might forget.

4 I'm learning English .... that I can study in Britain.

5 I'm going out .... buy some bread.

6 My brother and I don't speak to .... other very much.

7 Don't leave me here .... myself!

8 Sometimes I like to go to the theatre .... my own.

9 'Oh, dear! Have you hurt ....?' 'No, it's all right. I'm OK.'

10 They enjoy .... another's company enormously.

10

D Complete the gaps with one of the alternatives in brackets.

1 If you've got a headache, why don't you try ...... an aspirin? (taking/to take/take)

2 Can you smell something ......? (cook/to cook/cooking)

3 We had to stop ...... some milk on the way home. (get/getting/to get)

4 I now regret ...... so much money yesterday. (spending/to spend/spend)

5 He said hello and then went on ...... why he had come. (say/to say/saying)

5

E Rewrite the sentences with the word(s) in brackets.

1 You shouldn't stay up too late. (better) ....

2 She should buy some new clothes. (ought) ....

3 Turn off the light! (think/could) ....

4 Don't drive so fast! (would/mind) ....

5 Call a taxi. (wondering/could) ....

6 I won't go out because he might call. (in case) ....

7 We'd prefer to stay at home. (rather) ....

8 I'd sooner you left now. (prefer/if) ....

9 It isn't necessary for us to stand. (need) ....

10 Make an effort to be calm. (try) ....

10

F Correct the mistakes.

1 Shakespeare <u>has written</u> at least 35 plays. ....

2 I went to Italy <u>for to learn</u> Italian. ....

3 Please don't forget <u>watering</u> the plants when we're away. ....

4 The fridge was empty. Our guests <u>had been eating</u> everything. ....

5 You <u>mustn't</u> pay to get into the museum. It's free. ....

5

TOTAL

50

21 As long as you're careful

We use the zero conditional for things that are always true. (if = when)

If/When + present	+ present
If/When you **press** this switch,	the TV **comes** on.

We use the first conditional for events/situations that may or may not happen.

If + present	+ modal (*will, may* etc), *going to*, imperative
If it's cold tonight,	I'**ll** light a fire./ I'**m going to** stay in./**don't** go out!

ⓘ We can also use *as long as, provided that, even if, unless, only if, whether or not* to introduce conditions.
I'll cook dinner **as long as/provided that/only if** you do the washing up.
He won't go to the party **even if/whether or not** he's invited.
Unless I/If I don't wear glasses, I can't see a thing.

ⓘ We can use this conditional for promises, predictions, permission and warnings.
(**Unless** you…)

We use the second conditional for unlikely or imaginary situations in the present or future.

If + past	+ would/could/might
If you **went** to Canada, (unlikely but possible)	you **might** improve your English.
If I **were/was** rich, (I'm not rich)	I **wouldn't** work.

A Underline the correct answers.

1 In Saudi Arabia, **even if/provided that** it's very hot, men should wear a full business suit.

2 Americans might say 'Let's do lunch', but don't expect an invitation **if/unless** they say when!

3 In China, **if/even if** you are the guest of honour at a dinner, no one will leave before you.

4 In India, **if/unless** you are offered tea or a soft drink, it's impolite to refuse.

5 In the UK, **if/as long as** you're invited to a colleague's home, don't talk about business **if/unless** your host starts the conversation.

6 **Even if/Provided that** you only know a few words, Russians welcome any attempt to speak their language.

7 In Japan, don't be surprised **if/provided that** there are periods of silence during meetings.

8 **As long as/When** you get into a lift in Germany, you should say 'hello' to the other people in it.

B Write the verbs in the correct form.

1 If you _____touch_____ (touch) another person,
you _____should apologise_____ (apologise)
immediately.

2 _____ (be) on time for meetings, even
if you _____ (know) the other person
will be late.

3 Provided that it _____ (be) good quality, a small gift _____
(be/always) appreciated.

4 You _____ (shake) hands, as long as you _____ (not/grip)
too hard.

5 Never _____ (call) a business person at home unless it _____ (be)
an emergency.

C Complete the sentences for you. You can use one of the verbs in brackets.

1 If someone invites me to dinner, _____I always take a gift._____ (take a gift/be late)

2 Unless I know someone very well, _____
(use first names/touch)

3 Even if I know someone quite well, _____
(kiss/ask personal questions)

4 I think it is OK to _____ provided that
_____ (be late/dress casually)

D Continue these sentences using the words in brackets.

1 It would be much quicker if we _____flew direct to Luxor_____ . (fly/direct/Luxor)

2 You _____ to Egypt unless
_____ a visa. (not/travel; you/have)

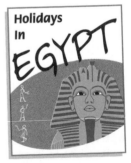

Holidays
in
EGYPT

3 What a pity! If we _____ , we could take
a Nile cruise. (have/more time)

4 We _____ by 6.00p.m. as long as the plane
_____ delayed. (be/there; not/be)

5 If we went to Aswan, we _____ to Kom
Ombo for the day. (get)

6 If I _____ you, I _____ to
the Red Sea and do some scuba diving! (be; go)

7 We can play golf near the Great Pyramids if we _____ in Cairo! (stay)

22 I'm getting used to it

be/get used to

	be	+ used to	+ noun/-ing
I	'm (not)	used to	the noise/getting up early. (= (not) accustomed
He	wasn't		to a new situation)
	get	+ used to	+ noun/-ing
She	's getting	used to	British food/working late (= becoming accustomed to)
	's got/got		**not** working very hard.

ⓘ Compare: I **used to like** (*used to* + infinitive) football but I don't now.

A Underline the correct form.

1 He got used to wear/<u>wearing</u>   2 I used to be/being   3 She didn't use to spend/spending   4 They aren't used to eat/eating   5 We can't get used to work/working   6 Did you use to swim/swimming?

B What things do you have to get used to? Complete the sentences in any way you like.

1 When you get married you have to *get used to sharing your life with someone.*

2 If you suddenly become famous you have to ....

3 When you retire you have to ....

4 When you first leave home you have to ....

5 When you have a baby you have to ....

C Use the correct form of *used to* to complete this letter.

The weather in New Zealand is very pleasant – even the winters are mild – and it didn't take me long to (1) *get used to having* (have) my summer in December! Luckily, I'm meeting lots of people, although I'm not sure I'll ever (2) .... (speak) English all the time. Travelling here is easy – the roads are great – but it's taking me a while to (3) .... (drive) on the left. On the farm we get up very early and go to bed very late but my father (4) .... (be) a farmer and I (5) .... (work) long hours. The thing I miss most about home is the food. I (6) .... (not/eat) bland food – I (7) .... spicy food! – but little by little I (8) .... it. Overall, I love my new life. Why don't you come out and stay for a few weeks?

23 The film's about to finish

Future forms

To talk about planned or fixed events we use
- *going to:* **I'm going to** get a new job. I'm tired of this one. (already decided/an intention)
- present continuous: **I'm seeing** the doctor tomorrow. (personal arrangement already made)
- present simple: My French classes **finish** next week. (public timetable/programme)
- *be to:* The Queen **is to** visit Canada next year. (formal official arrangements)
- *be due to:* The shop is **due to** open at 9.00. (expected to happen at a particular time)

To talk about unplanned events we use *will/shall:*
Wait. **I'll** help you. (spontaneous decision: offers, promises, requests, refusals)

To talk about predictions we use
- *going to:* **She's going to** have a baby. (we can see now that it is certain to happen)
- *will/shall:* Tom **will** fail his driving test. (personal opinion based on our experience)

To talk about events that are close to happening we use *about to:*
Our visitors are (just) **about to** leave. (soon, but not a specific time)

To talk about how sure we are about something (probability) we use
- *be (un)likely to:* The country's **likely to** get richer next year.
- *think/expect, be sure,* modals: I **think/expect/'m sure** we'll be late. We **might** be late.

A Replace the words in italics with one of the phrases in brackets in the correct form.

1 The club ~~will~~ _is to_ spend $100 million on a new stadium. (be likely to/be to)

2 The directors *are expected to* .... make an announcement shortly. (be about to/be due to)

3 The manager *will soon* .... buy some new players. (be about to/be likely to)

4 The team *will probably* .... do very well this year. (be to/be likely to)

5 The manager *is expected to* .... talk to the press later. (be due to/be likely to)

6 He *will* .... make an important announcement. (be to/be about to)

B Underline the correct form.

1 I'm free on Saturday. I **won't work/<u>'m not working</u>**.

2 I've decided to go to the match. I'**ll get/'m going to get** a ticket later.

3 Do you want to come with me? I **take/'m taking** the car.

4 Don't worry about buying a ticket. I'**m going to get/'ll get** one for you at the same time.

5 We can leave about 12. We'**ll be/'re going to be** there by 2.00.

6 That's plenty of time. The match **isn't starting/doesn't start** until 3.00.

7 Both teams have good players. It'**s about to be/'s going to be** a great match!

C **Write the verbs in the correct form, using negatives where necessary.**

1 (I hear you *'re going* (1) (go) to the beach later this morning.)

(Yes, we .... (2) (meet) some friends there.)

(According to the forecast, the weather .... (3) (be) lovely today.
I'm sure you .... (4) (have) a good time.)

2 (I .... (5) (take) Harika to the race on Saturday. Do you want to come?)

(What time .... (6) (start)?)

(At 3.00.)

(It .... (7) (be) a bit difficult. My meeting .... (8)
(due to/finish) till 2.30.)

3 (I must rush. Nadia .... (9) (fly) to New York on business in a few
hours and she .... (10) (about to/leave) for the airport. I'd like to
get home to say goodbye.)

(You'd better hurry. The roads .... (11) (be) very crowded at this
time of night.)

(OK. Bye. I .... (12) (see) you tomorrow.)

D **What would you say in these situations? Use a future form.**

1 You're talking about when you retire. *I'm going to take up photography.*
2 The phone rings. You offer to answer it. ....
3 You want to know the time of the last train. ....
4 You say what you've decided to buy your father for his birthday. ....
5 You're talking about the President's next visit to the UK. ....
6 You're talking about your diary for next week. ....
7 It's very cold and the sky has suddenly gone dark. ....
8 You're predicting the result of the next match. ....
9 You're talking about life in a 100 years time. ....

24 There aren't nearly as many

Countable nouns e.g. *people, bags, cars* etc.	Uncountable nouns e.g. *bread, luggage, time* etc.
so many/few; far more/fewer; many more; (not) (nearly) as many	*so much/little; far more/less; much more; (not) (nearly) as much*
There were **so many/so few** people there. It was awful.	There was **so much/so little** time (that) we didn't know what to do.
There were **far more/far fewer** people there than last year.	There was **far more/far less** time than we had expected.
There were **many more** people there than last year.	There was **much more** time than we had expected.
There aren't **(nearly) as many** cars as there were yesterday.	I haven't got **(nearly) as much** luggage as I thought.

ⓘ In the negative we can also say *not* **so** *much/many as...* but *not* **as** is more common.

A Underline the correct answer.

1 We've had **so much/so many/as many** rain this year. Everything's soaked.

2 I think we've had **so many/as much/so much** snow as last year, if not more.

3 There have been **so little/so few/as many** sunny days. I hope the weather improves.

4 I don't agree. There have been **far more/far less/nearly as much** fine days than last year.

5 There has been **much more/far fewer/so many** sunshine.

6 We haven't had **so much/far less/as many** storms.

B Complete the sentences.

1 There aren't _as many_ good bands as there were last year.

2 I've seen so _____ happy faces. It's wonderful!

3 Why are there far _____ police this year? There should be more.

4 There's so _____ good music to enjoy. Everyone has a good time.

5 There's far _____ exotic food for sale than I expected. I'm a bit disappointed.

6 It didn't cost me nearly _____ money to get here this year. I came by coach.

7 There aren't nearly _____ wonderful costumes as I was expecting.

8 There's so _____ excitement here. I love it.

25 Who else?

where/what/who/how/when/why + *else*?		
What/Who/How	*else*	do you know? (*else* = other thing/more)
When/Where/Why		would you go?

some(-one), any(-one), no(-one), every(-one) + *else*	
some(-one/-body/-thing/-where)	
any(-one/-body/-thing/-where)	+ *else*
no(-one/-body/-thing/-where)	
every(-one/-body/-thing/-where)	

We haven't got **anywhere else** to go. (= any other place) **Everybody else** is out.

ⓘ *else* has a possessive form: That's **somebody else's** jacket.

ⓘ There is no plural form: some other people NOT ~~some people else~~

ⓘ We cannot say: ~~Which else…? Whose else…?~~

A Complete the interview with a detective. Use a question word, or a *some-*, *any-*, *no-*, *every-* word, with *else*.

1 The woman in the flat above was at home but
   everyone else was out.

2 '_____ had a front door key?' 'No-one.'

3 'Did you leave the wallet _____ by
   mistake?' 'No, nowhere. I'm sure I didn't.'

4 '_____ knew where the money was.
   Only me.'

5 '_____ did they take?' 'Nothing. Just the money.'

6 '_____ did you go last night?' 'Nowhere. Just the cinema.'

7 There was _____ car parked outside when I left. I don't know whose
   it was. It didn't belong to anyone here.

8 'Have you got _____ to say?' 'No, nothing.'

B Complete the sentences with *else* and any other words you need.

1 ' _Who else_ had a key?' 'Tanya did.'

2 _____ broke the window. It wasn't me.

3 '_____ did the woman upstairs say?' 'She also said that she was going
   away for the weekend.'

4 I haven't looked in the car but I've looked _____ .

5 _____ could the robber have got in? Through the window?

6 I went to the cinema because I had _____ to do.

7 'Have you spoken to _____ about the robbery?' 'No, just you.'

26 Don't make a noise!

do or make?

We use *do* + *the/some* + noun/*-ing* to talk about repeated activities e.g. at work/home:
We **did the/some exercise/work/shopping/cleaning/cooking/driving**.

We use *do* + *something/nothing* + *for/to/about* to talk about taking action:
We must **do something about** the problem. She's **done something to** her hair. (changed)
What can I **do for** you? (how can I help?)

ⓘ We use *do* to describe a process/general activity: What are you **doing**? That's **done**!

ⓘ We also use *do* in fixed expressions: + *good/well/your best, exercise, a favour, overtime*

We use *make* + object + adjective/verb when something causes something to happen:
That film **makes me sad/laugh**.

make + noun (become): The garage would **make a good office**.

ⓘ We can use *make* in fixed expressions (= create): + *an appointment, money, noise, plans, a cup of tea*

A Complete the sentences with *make* or *do* in the correct form.

1 'I'm sorry you can't see the director. You'll have to _make_ an appointment.'

2 'You must _____ something about the state of your office. It's a mess!'

3 'Have you _____ any plans for the weekend?'
'No, none.'

4 'You've been _____ a lot of overtime recently.'
'I know. We've got a big project on.'

5 'Could you _____ us all a cup of coffee?'
'All right. I won't be a minute.'

6 'Could you _____ me a favour?'
'I'll _____ my best.'

7 'Why haven't you _____ the filing?'
'You'd _____ a good manager. You're always telling me what to do!'

B Complete the sentences for you using *do* or *make*.

1 _One of my customers made_ me quite angry last week.

2 I think _____ too much noise.

3 _____ the shopping _____ .

4 _____ a lot of money.

5 _____ things for other people.

6 _____ exercise after work tomorrow.

27 I invited them to stay

	verb	+ object/person	+ to-infinitive
He	taught/got	me	to swim.
I	reminded/warned	her	(not) to book early.

verb + object + to-infinitive   **verb + object + -ing**

Other verbs: *expect, mean, intend, invite, order, recommend, take (ages)*

	verb	+ object/person	+ -ing
We	saw/can't imagine	him	cleaning the floor.

Other verbs: *dislike/not like, involve, keep, mind, prevent, stop, spend (time/money)*

A **A tennis player is talking about a recent course. Complete the sentences with verb + object + -ing or to- infinitive.**

TENNIS ACADEMY TRAINING SCHEDULE
* work on your fitness in the mornings
* take part in practice matches every afternoon
* don't miss the daily meetings with your coach
* discuss videos of your practice matches
* don't play in the evenings
* take Saturdays off
* don't train too hard

1 They (get) _got me to work_ on my fitness in the mornings.

2 They (expect) _____ practice matches every afternoon.

3 They (not/like) _____ the daily meetings with my coach.

4 The meetings (involve) _____ videos of my practice matches.

5 They (stop) _____ in the evenings.

6 They (not/mind) _____ Saturdays off.

7 They (warn) _____ too hard.

B **Complete the sentences. Use the words in brackets.**

1 They taught (the boy/play) _the boy to play_ tennis.

2 We can't imagine (Ivan/get up) _____ at 8am every morning.

3 It took (me/ages/find) _____ the place.

4 Can you remind (him/buy) _____ some new shoes?

5 We can't prevent (him/go) _____ out with his friends.

6 I've spent (a lot of time/try) _____ to improve his technique.

28 He works as a waiter

as/like

as

We can use *as* + noun to describe what someone does: He works **as a hotel receptionist**.

We use *as* + clause to mean *in the same way*: He arrived late, (just) **as** I said he would.

Prices are very high, **as** (they were) **in** the 1990s. (*as* + preposition) **As** you know, my exam is tomorrow. (= you know this already) **As** it was late, I decided.... (= Because) **As** I was walking up the road, I saw... (= While)

like

We use *like* + noun/pronoun to mean 'in a similar way': He plays golf (very much/a bit) **like a beginner**. (similar to a beginner)

ⓘ We also use *like* (or *such as*) to give examples: He prefers classical composers, **like/such as** Beethoven.

like/as if (as though)

We use *like* + noun/pronoun or *as if* + clause after verbs like *feel, look, seem, sound, smell* and *treat* (+ object):
It **looks/feels like** rain. It **looks/feels as if (though)** it's going to rain.
They treat me **like** their son. They treat me **as if/though I were** their son.

ⓘ In colloquial English we use *like* + clause after *feel, look* etc.
It **looks/feels like it's going to** rain.

A Complete the gaps with *as* or *like*.

ADVENTURE TREK! *action holidays*

1 After university I had a job ..*as*.. a travel guide for several months.

2 On the website it was described .... an adventure trek.

3 .... a climb it wasn't very high, but it was difficult. I wouldn't take risks .... that now.

4 There was heavy snow – .... in the previous year according to local people.

5 I behaved .... a fool and we got lost. My feet were .... ice – they were freezing.

6 .... I expected, I couldn't get a signal on my mobile phone.

7 We worked .... a team and did things .... trying to light a fire. Everyone did .... I asked them to do.

8 .... everyone else in the group, I found it a very long night!

B Combine the two sentences with *as*.

1 They were looking for us. I expected that. *As I expected, they were looking for us.*

2 I couldn't sleep. The reason was I was worried. ....

3 I woke up early. I knew I would. ....

4 We were getting up. We heard a noise. ....

5 They found us. I said they would. ....

C Underline the correct alternative.

1 You sound **as/as if** you could do with a rest.

2 Why do you talk to me **as/as if** I were a child?

3 I wish I could speak Swahili **as/like** you.

4 He looks **like/as** he is going to be sick.

5 Don't touch! Leave things exactly **as/as if** they are.

6 They treated me **as/like** a hero, but I wasn't really.

7 She behaves **as/as if** she **is/were** much older than she really is.

8 **As/As if** we can't meet tomorrow, let's make a date for next week.

D Complete the sentences. Use the words in brackets and *as/like/as if/as though*.

1 You look terrible. You (look/you've seen/a ghost) *look as if you've seen a ghost*

2 What are you cooking? It (smell/Indian food) ....

3 This is horrible. It (taste/it's made of cardboard) ....

4 What's that noise? It (sound/thunder) ....

5 What a lot of mess! It (look/a bomb's hit it) ....

E Complete the letter with *as*, *like* or *as if*.

At the moment I'm working (1) _as_ a voluntary
teacher in Uganda. (2) .... with any voluntary work, I
don't get paid but I do get things (3) .... free
accommodation and travel expenses. When I first saw
the job advertised, it seemed (4) .... a good idea but
I didn't realise how difficult it was going to be. At the
beginning my students looked at me (5) .... I were
crazy and I felt (6) .... I wasn't achieving very much. However, (7) .... everyone
kept telling me I would, I've started to really enjoy the work. All of us in the school
work hard and (8) .... our students are really bright, the progress they've made has
been fantastic. Really, this work is (9) .... nothing I've ever experienced before.
Why don't you try it sometime?

29 I hope so

so

We can use *so* to avoid repeating a phrase:
- after 'opinion' verbs like *expect, guess, hope, imagine, (it) seems, suppose, think, I'm afraid.*
'Do you agree with me?' 'I suppose/think **so**.' (I suppose/think I agree with you.)
- after *say* and *tell* (+ object).
'You're mad!' 'Who says **so**?' (Who says I'm mad?) 'It's a terrible film.' 'I told you **so**.'

In the negative:
- we prefer *not... so* with *expect, imagine, think.* I **don't** expect **so**. I wouldn't imagine **so**.
- we use *not* after *I'm afraid, guess, hope.* I'm afraid **not**. I hope **not**.
- we can use either *don't...so* or *not* after *(it) seems, suppose.* It doesn't seem **so**/seems **not**.

ⓘ We don't usually say: ~~I know so. I'm sure so.~~

ⓘ 'Are you hungry? If **so** (If you are hungry), let's get something to eat. If **not**, let's do some more work.'

A Write *so* or *not* in the gaps.

1 'Are you going to the meeting?' 'Yes, I suppose __so__ .'

2 'Do I have to go?' 'I imagine _____ . All managers are expected to attend.'

3 'Is there an agenda?' 'I don't think _____ .'

4 'Will the meeting go on all day?' 'I hope _____ . I've got a lot to do.'

5 'Is the meeting about our production plans?' 'Yes, it seems _____ .'

6 'Apparently, we've got a new design.' 'Who says _____ ?'

7 'Are we all going out for lunch?' 'I'm afraid _____ . We're too busy.'

8 Is Kim going to the meeting? If _____ , can she go to the bank for me?

B Complete the answers in the positive or negative.

1 'Are we going to get new premises?' (expect) ' __I expect so__ . These are too small.'

2 'Will we need to borrow money?' (guess) '_____ . We usually do.'

3 'Is there a market for the product?' (hope) '_____ . Our future depends on it!'

4 'Can I take on a lot of new staff?' (afraid) '_____ . We can't afford it.'

5 'Haven't other companies got the same idea?' (imagine) '_____ . It's very original.'

6 'We don't need more market research, do we?' (guess) '_____ . We've already done a lot.'

7 'The meeting was about future plans.' (tell/you) 'I _____ ! Was it interesting?'

30 She said she had seen him

How we report speech depends on when and where the speakers were talking. We often change tenses, pronouns and some verbs and time and place words. For example:

'I'm at home today.' → She said (that) **she was** at home **that** day.
'I've been here before.' → He said (that) **he had been there** before.
'Don't bring any money.' → He **told me not to take** any money.
'I saw him yesterday.' → She said (that) **she had seen** him **the day before**.
'Do you like this music?' He asked me **if/whether I liked that** music. (*yes/no* questions)
'How old is he?' She asked me/wanted to know **how old he was.** (*wh-/how* questions)
'I'll help you tomorrow.' → He said that **he would** help **me the next/following day**.
'I'm coming later.' → She said (that) **she was going** later.
'I saw it last week.' → He said (that) he**'d seen** it **the previous week**.

ⓘ *can* → *could*; *must* → *had to*; *may* → *might*

ⓘ He said (that) he **wants** to see me **tomorrow**. (it is still true)

ⓘ We do not change the past perfect or the modals *would, should, might, could, ought to*.

A Write a word or phrase we can use when we report these words.

1 here *there*   2 tomorrow ....   3 yesterday ....

4 coming ....   5 today ....   6 this ....   7 have ....

8 will ....   9 must ....   10 may ....

B Write the direct speech.

1 He asked me if I could help with the cooking.

> *Can you help with the cooking?*

2 He wanted to know how well I could cook.

3 I said I had been trained by a top chef.

4 He asked me to give him some ideas for the meal.

5 I told him not to worry. We would think of something.

C Underline the correct alternative.

1 They **told/said** me they **have enjoyed/had enjoyed** the meal.

2 I **said/told** to them that I **am/was** very pleased.

3 They asked **me/to me** where **I had/had I** learnt to cook so well.

4 They wanted to know whether **would I/I would/I will/will I** cook the next day.

5 I asked him **that he should phone/to phone** me the next day if he **needed/had needed** me.

D A receptionist is telling a doctor phone messages on Monday morning. Complete the sentences. Change tenses and other words as necessary.

1 'I must see the doctor urgently. I need advice about my diet.'
He said *he must see you urgently. He needs advice about his diet.*

2 'I'm sorry I can't get there on Monday. Can I see the doctor another day?'
He said ....
He wanted to know ....

3 'I'll phone back later.'
He said ....

4 'Will the doctor want to see my medical records?'
She asked ....

5 'What would be the best time to see the doctor next week?'
He wanted to know ....

6 'Phone me as soon as the doctor gets in on Monday morning.'
She asked ....

E These people are reporting their meeting with a dietician last week. Complete the gaps. Report the sentences, changing tenses and other words as necessary.

Is drinking coffee bad for me?

How many cups do you drink a day?

I have about four large cups in the morning.

That's too much coffee. Try to drink more water.

1 I wanted to know *if drinking coffee was bad for me* and she asked
.... I told ....
about four large cups in the morning but she said
.... and told ....

What did you have for lunch last week?

I ate meat every day.

Did you eat any green vegetables?

I had a salad one day.

2 She asked me .... and I said
.... Then she wanted to know
.... and I told ....

Test 3 (Units 21–30)

A Circle the correct answer.

1 You can come as long as you **don't bring/won't bring** your sister.

2 I **got used to/used to** swim a lot when I was younger.

3 He's **due to/about to** start school next autumn.

4 There are **far/much** more flowers than there were this time last year.

5 I don't like that dress. Have you got **anything/anything else** to wear?

6 Have you **made/done** the shopping yet?

7 They warned us not **to step/stepping** on the ice.

8 **As/Like** you can see, I'm very busy.

9 'Are you going to work later?' 'I **suppose/suppose so**.'

10 He said that he **has spoken/had spoken** to her earlier.

10

B Write the correct form of the verb.

1 Even if they .... (score) a goal, they'll still lose.

2 I .... (not/get) the tickets unless you .... (call) me. OK?

3 If she .... (be) in love with him, she .... (marry) him, but she isn't.

4 It took me ages to get used to .... (work) at night.

5 I'm not used to .... (live) in hot countries.

6 I can't see you tomorrow. I .... (play) golf.

7 The doctor's not here but I expect he .... (be) back later.

8 They invited us .... (stay) for the weekend.

9 I can't imagine her .... (criticise) other people.

10 She said she .... (like) to see us tomorrow.

10

C Complete the gaps with one word.

1 Where is everyone? There are far .... people here than I expected.

2 There's .... much information in this encyclopaedia. It's amazing.

3 Of course I gave them the money. What .... could I do?

4 'Is the car park full?' 'I hope .... I've got to get some shopping.'

5 'Will he mind if I borrow his laptop?' 'I don't think ....'

5

D Make sentences using the words in brackets in the correct form.

1 He's very popular. (tickets/likely/be/expensive) ....

2 Hurry up! (the film/about/start) ....

3 They ordered (me/take off) .... my coat.

4 The job involves (me/travel) .... all over the country.

5 Stop those people (take) .... photographs.

5

E Complete the gaps with the correct alternative.

1 We haven't spent .... money as you. (nearly as many/nearly as much)

2 There's .... milk in the fridge. (so little/so few)

3 .... knew except me. (anybody else/nobody else)

4 You're good at maths. You'd .... a good accountant. (make/do)

5 When I saw her after 20 years, she felt .... a stranger. (as/like)

5

F Report the sentences, changing tenses and other words as necessary.

1 'I've mended the door.' He said he ....

2 'Do you like our flat?' They asked me ....

3 'What are you doing tomorrow?' I asked her ....

4 'You must come and see me.' He said that I ....

5 'Don't move this picture!' He told me ....

5

G Correct the mistakes.

1 If I <u>don't have</u> a car, I couldn't get to work. ....

2 We soon got used to <u>live</u> in the city. ....

3 Have you heard the news? Tom <u>will be</u> sacked! ....

4 <u>What would you like else?</u> ....

5 After work tonight I'm going to <u>make</u> some exercise. ....

6 It was a sad film. It made me <u>to cry</u>. ....

7 He doesn't like <u>that you go</u> there without me. ....

8 It sounds <u>as</u> you had a good time. ....

9 She's good at ball sports, <u>as</u> tennis. ....

10 'It's getting late.' 'I <u>know so</u>.' ....

10

TOTAL

50

31 She was going to tell him but ...

was/were going to + infinitive; was/were planning to + infinitive		
I	**was going to** **was planning to**	**email** her last night but I forgot. (past plan/intention)
was/were thinking of + -ing		
They	**were thinking of**	**walking** but they changed their mind and went by bus.
(be) about to + infinitive		
We	**were (just) about to**	**go out** when the phone rang. (very soon)
(be) due to + infinitive		
I	**was due to**	**go** to the doctor last Monday, but I had to cancel. (an arranged event)

ⓘ We can also use *was/were going to* for past predictions. I thought it **was going to be** really cold, but it isn't.

A Underline the correct alternatives.

1 The match **was about to/due to** start at 3.00pm but the players arrived late.

2 I was **thinking of buying/due to buy** a CD, but I didn't have enough money.

3 The thief was **about to/due to** steal the watch when he saw a security guard looking at him.

4 We were **about to/due to** fly to Italy next month, but the trip was cancelled.

5 I thought the course was **planning to/going to** be really interesting but it wasn't. It was dull.

6 I was **planning to/due to** ask my manager for a day off but I saw she was in a terrible mood.

B Complete the gaps in these news stories with the expressions in brackets and the verb in the correct form.

1

A well-known author was just (move) *about to move* house when he decided to burn some old papers. He did it very quickly because the removal company was (arrive) _____ in 10 minutes. Unfortunately, the poor man also burnt the original manuscript of his first book, worth over £100,000.
(about to/due to)

2

A young footballer had had his shirt signed by his favourite team. He was (put) _____ it away somewhere safe when he got home but he forgot. Unfortunately, when his mother saw the | shirt, she thought it was dirty. That evening, just as he was (go) _____ to bed, to his horror, he saw a clean shirt hanging up in the wardrobe.
(thinking of/planning to)

32 I wish I knew

wish

wish + past (for imaginary situations in the present)

I	wish	I **had**	a new car. (I'm not happy with my old one.)
		I **was/were**	younger. (I don't like being old but I am.)
		he **didn't**	spend so much money. (Unfortunately, he does.)
		the sun **was**	shining. (Unfortunately, it's cloudy.)
		he **could**	swim. (But he can't. *could* = have the ability)
		I **could**	go to the cinema. (But I probably can't. *could* = be possible)

wish + you/she/he/they would

I	wish	**you would**	stop talking. (I want you to stop but you don't = criticism/complaint)
		she wouldn't	work so hard. (I want her to work less.)

ⓘ *I wish I were...* is a little more formal than *I wish I was...*

ⓘ We use *would* for reasonable actions, not impossible situations. I wish you **would** hurry up! I wish you **were** younger. NOT I wish you ~~would be~~ younger.

ⓘ *If only = I wish* but is a little stronger. **If only I had** a new car! **If only you wouldn't** work so hard!

Ⓐ Underline the correct alternative in these children's wishes.

1 I wish I **would have/<u>had</u>** a video player in my room. I would lie in bed and watch films all day.

2 I wish I **was/would be** a rock star because I'd like to be famous.

3 I wish I **could/would** be a professional model for a day. It would be fantastic!

4 I wish I **had/have** a horse and **could/would** ride really well.

5 I wish I **am/were** a magician. I would play tricks on my family.

6 If only I **met/could meet** and dance with a famous ballerina some day.

Ⓑ Put the verbs in the correct form and complete the sentences for you.

1 I wish I (have) *had a swimming pool at home*.

2 I wish I (be) _____ because _____.

3 I wish today (be) _____ because _____.

4 I wish I (can) _____ in the mornings.

5 If only I (can) _____!

C Write sentences using the words in brackets.

1 She sometimes wishes (she/not/be/) ...... *she weren't* ...... so famous.

2 If only (the press/leave/him) .... alone!

3 He wishes (more people/try) .... and understand him.

4 They wish (the newspapers/not invent) .... untrue stories about their life together.

5 She sometimes wishes (she/can lead) .... an ordinary life.

6 He wishes (he/not/have to spend) .... so much time in Hollywood.

7 He wishes (he/watch) .... cricket today!

D Complete the sentences.

1 It's very cold in here.
   I wish ...... *it weren't so cold in here* ....

2 My husband never helps with the cleaning.
   I wish ....

3 I never have time to read a book.
   I wish ....

4 I get a headache in the evenings.
   If only .... !

5 I have to go to work tomorrow.
   If only .... !

33 By the time he's finished

When we talk about the future, we can use different present forms after the following time words:

As soon as		
When	I receive/I've received	the tickets, I'll send them to you.
After		
Once		
While	you're having/you have	a shower, I'll cook dinner.

Other linking words: Don't move **until** I tell you. **By the time** you've finished college, you'll be over 21!

ⓘSometimes there is a difference in meaning between the present simple and present perfect: **When we have** dinner, I'll tell you something interesting. (at the same time) **When we've had** dinner, I'll tell you something interesting. (after dinner)

A Underline the correct alternative.

1 By the time **we're deciding/we've decided** on a holiday, the summer will be over!

2 After **you've looked/you're looking** at that brochure, I'll give it back to the assistant.

3 What will you do while **I'm making/I've made** the booking?

4 Once **I'll pay/I've paid** for the holiday, I'll meet you in the cafe.

5 We'll give Rana a ring as soon as **we get/we'll get** there.

6 We won't go and see her until **we check/we've checked** into the hotel.

7 We'll look at the map together when **we sit/we're sitting** on the plane.

B Join the sentences. Use the word in brackets.

1 You have a shower. I'll find Keiko's address. (while)
   While you're having a shower, I'll find Keiko's address.

2 I'll wait here. You get dressed first. (until)
   .... dressed.

3 The taxi will arrive soon. Then we must leave immediately. (once)
   .... immediately.

4 We'll see Keiko. After that we'll find somewhere to eat. (as soon as)
   .... somewhere to eat.

5 We'll get back home at 10.00. It'll be very dark. (by the time)
   .... very dark.

34 You must be joking!

When we are sure that something is (not) happening we can use:

	must/can't/couldn't	+ be	+ -ing	
He	**must/can't**	**be**	**waiting**	for his brother.

When we think it is possible that something is (not) happening we can use:

	may (not)/might (not)/could	+ be	+ -ing	
It	**may (not)/might (not)/could**	**be**	**raining.**	Let's go and see.

A Write the verb in the correct form.

1 'There's a lot of noise next door. Andreas and Anna must _be having_ (have) a party.'

'No, they can't _____ (have) a party. They went out with friends.'

2 'The children might _____ (rehearse) with their band. They have a concert tomorrow.'

'They could _____ (play) a computer game. There are a lot of strange noises.'

3 'You're always complaining. You must _____ (get) old!'

B Complete the sentences with *may/might/could*, *must* or *can't* and the correct form of the verb.

1 'Karel's bought a new car. He _must be doing_ (do) well.'

'Not necessarily. He _____ (get) a loan from the bank to pay for it.'

2 'Where's Nora? It's very late. She _____ (work) at this hour, surely.'

'I don't know. She _____ (visit) her mother. I'll phone and check.'

3 'The kids are unusually quiet. They _____ (watch) TV.'

'You never know. They _____ (do) their homework!'

4 'He says he's 40 but I'm not sure. He _____ (not/tell) the truth.'

'My guess is that he's 50. Whatever the truth, he _____ (do) much exercise. He looks so unfit.'

35 A new one

one/ones, the one/the ones, another one/other ones

	singular countable noun	(a/the)	+ adjective	+ one
'Would you like	a biscuit?'	'Yes, a	small	**one**, please.'
	plural countable noun	(the)	+ adjective	+ ones
'Would you like	some crisps?'	'Yes, (the)	plain	**ones**, please.'

Which	+ one(s)	the/this/that/these/those	+ one(s)
'Which	**one/ones** would you like?'	('The)	**one/ones** over there.'
		'This/That/The other/ Not that	**one**.'
		'These/Those	**(ones)**.'

'Would you like another **one**?/the other **ones**.' Yes, please.'

ⓘ We cannot use *a one*: **One** with chocolate on. A **big** one. NOT ~~A one with chocolate on.~~

ⓘ *one* cannot replace uncountable nouns: 'There's no water.' 'I'll get some.' NOT '...~~one~~'

ⓘ 'Have you got **a** coat?' 'Yes, I've got **one**.'
'Have you got **your** coat?' 'Yes, I've got it.' NOT '... ~~one.~~'

A Match the questions and answers.

1 Do you like this T-shirt? ___e___   a The dark ones.
2 Which jeans do you like best? _____   b The brown ones? Yes.
3 Which dress should I buy? _____   c Sure. Do you mean this one?
4 Have you seen those shoes? _____   d The more formal one, I think.
5 Can I see that suit? _____   e No, I want a more fashionable one.

B Complete the sentences with *one/ones, the one/the ones, another one/the other ones*.

1 'Look at those boots!' 'Which ___ones___ do you mean?'

2 'Which skirt do you prefer?' '_____ over there with the leather belt.'

3 'I'm going to buy a winter coat.' '_____ ? I thought you already had _____ ?'

4 'What sort of trainers are you looking for?' '_____ without laces.'

5 'I need some new shoes.' 'Do you like _____ over there with very high heels?'

6 'These are too small.' 'Do you want to try _____ ?'

7 'I've already got a cardigan.' 'It doesn't matter. Get _____ . This is a good price!'

36 I remember a time when ...

A Write *whose, where* or *when* in the gaps.

1 We are a company ___*whose*___ clients include many international banks.

2 I can't remember a time _____ we've had so many orders.

3 This is the department _____ main job is to support our many overseas customers.

4 Are you staying in the hotel _____ we had our exhibition last year?

5 We have offices in many cities _____ the population is increasing dramatically.

6 July's the month _____ we usually have to increase production.

B Join the sentences with *whose, where* or *when*.

1 It's a good company. Its name is known throughout the world.
It's a *good company whose name is known* throughout the world.

2 They do the job very quickly. I don't know any other company like this.
I don't know any other company _____ so quickly.

3 Their head office is in an Asian country. Its economy is growing rapidly.
Their head office is in _____ rapidly.

4 Tomorrow's the day. We have to make a final decision then.
Tomorrow's _____ a final decision.

5 I know a restaurant. We can get a really good meal there.
I know _____ a really good meal.

37 My car, which is new, ...

Non-defining relative clauses

who (for people)

My father, **who** lives in Poland, is 91. (My father lives in Poland. He is 91.)

which (for things)

The phone, **which** had been quiet all evening, suddenly rang.

whose (for possession)

Rita, **whose** mother is a scientist, got very good results in her exams.

where (for places)

He went on holiday to Greece, **where** he spent a week sunbathing.

when (for time)

You should come on Monday, **when** the museum is open.

ⓘRelative clauses can also add information to the whole sentence, not just the nouns:
She was ill, **which** was very unusual for her.

A Complete these extracts from a guidebook.

1 Songkran, *which* is Thailand's most important festival, takes place in April.

2 April's a good time to have the festival, ... it's very hot.

3 This religious festival, ... marks the beginning of Solar Year, is celebrated with water.

4 Thai people, ... are very friendly and hospitable, throw water at each other.

5 Phuket Island, ... many foreign visitors spend their holidays, is particularly exciting.

6 Foreign tourists, ... cameras can get very wet, are often surprised by the festivities.

7 People buy fish and birds and set them free, ... they hope will bring them good fortune.

8 In Paklat, women in traditional dress carry the fish in bowls to the river, ... they are released.

B Join the sentences. Use the word in brackets.

1 Thailand has never been governed by a foreign country. Its people are 95% Buddhist. (whose)
   Thailand, whose people are 95% Buddhist, has never been governed by a foreign country.

2 Thailand changed its name in 1939. It used to be known as Siam. (which)

3 The King has ruled since 1946. He is called 'The Great' by his people. (who)

4 July can be quite uncomfortable. The rainy season begins then. (when)

5 The best time to go is February. This is when the weather is at its best. (which)

6 Chiang Mai is in the north of the country. You can buy beautiful handicrafts there. (where)

C Make one sentence using the extra information in brackets.

1 Last year I went to stay with my best friend. (He lives in Australia.)
   Last year I went to stay with my best friend, who lives in Australia.

2 Unfortunately, he's married to Karen. (I don't like her very much.)

3 We flew from Switzerland. (We were staying there for the summer.)

4 Melbourne is the cultural capital of Australia. (My friend has a house there.)

5 Tara came with us. (Her daughter has just moved to Australia.)

6 Spring is the best time to go. (There are flowers everywhere then.)

D Complete the sentences for you.

1 My mother, who ....

2 My mobile phone, which ....

3 July, when ....

4 He's never been on a plane before, which ....

5 My boss, whose ....

6 My favourite hotel, where ....

38 It was being repaired

Passive: *was being/had been* + past participle

	Past continuous	+ past participle	
My computer	**was (probably) being**	**repaired**	at the time.
	Past perfect	+ past participle	
The work	**had (only) been**	**finished**	the day before.

Verbs with two objects *(ask, bring, give, lend, offer, pay, promise, send, show, teach, tell)* have two possible passive structures:
Active: A friend gave me (person) the book (thing). → Passive: I (person) **was given** this book by a friend. OR This book (thing) **was given** to me by a friend.
Usually we make the person the subject of the sentence.

ⓘ We use the passive when we want to put new information at the end of a sentence for emphasis. I went to the party. I **had been invited** there **by my brother**.

ⓘ The passive can sound formal and impersonal and is more common in writing than speaking.

ⓘ We do not use the passive with
• verbs with no objects: NOT ~~It was arrived.~~
• state verbs such as *be, have* (= own), *seem*: NOT ~~A new car is being had by Jane.~~
• verbs of wanting and liking *(love, want, hate)*: He wanted her to go. NOT ~~She was wanted to go.~~

A Underline the correct alternative.

1 'Why was the man arrested?' 'Because he **had been seen**/**was being seen** breaking into a car.'

2 By the time the fire brigade got there, the factory **was being destroyed**/**had been destroyed** by the fire.

3 The children were still very upset and **had been comforted**/**were being comforted** by friends.

4 When she got back home, there was nobody there and all her jewellery **was being stolen**/**had been stolen**.

5 The education minister said that at the moment too many children **were being educated**/**had been educated** at home.

6 'Who did it?' 'We don't know but a man **had been questioned**/**was being questioned** by the police when I left.'

B Complete the sentences using a different passive form.

1 A big pay rise has been promised to all staff.
  All staff *have been promised a big pay rise.*

2 The foreign visitors will be shown the city's main attractions in the morning.
  The city's main attractions .... in the morning.

3 It seems that a lot of lies were told to the police.
  It seems that the police ....

4 A new agreement was being brought to the two parties to sign.
  The two parties ....

5 The finance director had been offered the job of general manager.
  The job of general manager ....

C Complete this news story with the verb in the correct form in the active or passive.

THE WORLD'S SMALLEST BABY

Last night the world's smallest baby was born in a hospital near Chicago. When the baby (1) *was weighed* (weigh) by staff it was under 250 grams, the weight of a can of cola. Last night doctors (2) .... (make) a statement to the press, saying that the baby (3) .... (be) in great danger and the parents (4) .... (not/allow) to hold her for the moment. They also said that a tube (5) .... (use) to give the baby food, but that she (6) .... (not/feed) by her mother yet.

D Complete the news story with a verb from the box in the correct form. Use the active or passive.

HOLIDAY COUPLE IN KIDNAP DRAMA

not/allow   ask   break down   eat   kidnap   not/know   ~~realise~~   refuse
rescue   rush in   take   tie (us) up   watch   want

"It was frightening. We soon (1) *realised* that our villa (2) .... nearly all the time. Then one evening, as we (3) .... dinner, our front door (4) .... and four men (5) .... carrying guns. They quickly (6) .... and we (7) .... to a remote part of the island. We (8) .... to phone our parents to tell them we (9) .... but of course we (10) .... At that time we (11) .... that our parents (12) .... to pay a large sum of money and that they (13) .... Luckily, though, after four days, we (14) .... by the police."

39 That's a good idea

To avoid repetition we can refer back to things by using:
• personal pronouns such as *they, her, its.*
I met your sister. **She**'s very nice.
• the definite article *the.*
She's got two children. **The** son is a teacher and **the** daughter is an engineer.
• determiners *(this, that, these, those).*
'Would you like to come round tomorrow?' '**That** sounds good.'
• *there/then.*
Cambridge is a lovely city. We stayed **there** last summer. It was very busy **then**.
• auxiliary verbs.
He promised to write and he **did/has/will**.

ⓘ For dramatic effect, we can use pronouns to refer forward to things:
When I first met **him**, Tom was working in a factory.
On **her** 18th birthday, Jane bought her first car.

A What do the words in bold refer to in this theatre review?

Othello – A tragedy by William Shakespeare

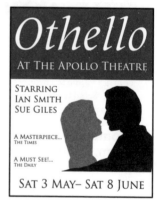

Othello
AT THE APOLLO THEATRE

STARRING
IAN SMITH
SUE GILES

A MASTERPIECE...
THE TIMES

A MUST SEE!...
THE DAILY

SAT 3 MAY– SAT 8 JUNE

'Othello' was first performed in 1604. (1) **It** is about a great soldier and his love for (2) **his** wife, Desdemona. In the play, Othello becomes jealous when Iago, an officer, suggests she is in love with the handsome soldier, Cassio. In a fit of anger he kills (3) **her**, and then, when (4) **he** realises his mistake, kills himself. Audiences are fascinated as they sit (5) **there** in the theatre, watching the tragedy develop. In (6) **this** production at the Apollo theatre, the performances are particularly intense. The actors are nearly always on stage so that when (7) **they** are not part of the action, they stand (8) **there** like statues looking at everything. I never expected them to be so good but they (9) **were**. When (10) **they** realised how exciting the play was, the teenage audience loved (11) **it** and so (12) **did** I.

1 *Othello – the play* 2 .... 3 ....
4 .... 5 .... 6 ....
7 .... 8 .... 9 ....
10 .... 11 .... 12 ....

B Complete the gaps with a word from the box.

did do it not ~~so~~ that them then there

1 'Are you going to see the play?' 'Yes, I think __so__.'
2 'Do you like his plays?' 'Yes, I like _____ a lot.'
3 'What do you think of 'Othello'?' 'I've never seen _____.'
4 'When will you get to the theatre?' 'I'll be _____ at 8 o'clock.' 'OK. I'll see you
_____.'
5 'It's a good production.' 'Who told you _____?' 'Nick _____.'
6 'Will you have dinner first?' 'I might _____ but I might _____.'

C Complete these extracts from a magazine article. Do not repeat the words in brackets.

1 The Spice Girls were a British pop group of the 1990s who talked about Girl
Power. (Girl Power) _It/That_ was an
idea that was very popular at (during the
1990s) _____ time.

2 The girls decided they were going to sell
a lot of records and (the girls sold a lot of
records) _____.

3 (The Spice Girls') _____ best songs
are probably the early (songs) _____.

4 After (the Spice Girls) _____ broke up, only Mel C and Emma had big hit
records. (They had big hit records) _____ is probably because they had better
voices.

5 Victoria married the footballer David Beckham in 1999. Since (1999) _____,
she has become even more of a celebrity.

D Rewrite the first sentence(s) so that the determiners and pronouns refer forward to things.

1 Nick entered a talent competition. He did this when he was twenty.
When _____he was twenty_____, Nick _entered a talent competition_.
2 The dancers looked incredible. They were wearing red trousers.
In _____, the dancers _____.
3 Tania went to California. She tried to get a job in the movies.
When _____, Tania _____.
4 Nobody could understand Rory. He had a strange accent.
With _____, nobody _____.
5 John left the company. I never saw him again.
After _____, I _____.

40 I'll learn how to cook

Indirect questions

I don't know	+ question word	+ subject	+ verb
	when	he	's coming.
	+ *if/whether*	+ subject	+ verb
	if/whether	she	has passed her test (or not).
	+ question word	+ *to-* infinitive	
	what	to do.	
	+ *whether*	+ *to-* infinitive	
	whether	to enter the competition.	

ⓘ We use *whether* (not *if*):
• immediately before *or not*.
I don't know **whether or not** she has passed her test.
• after a preposition.
I'm not clear **about whether** the car's safe enough to drive.

A Complete the sentences.

1 I never did discover ___*where*___ I left my car keys.
2 Sometimes I don't even remember _____ day it is.
3 I wonder _____ my memory will ever improve.
4 I've forgotten _____ to do. Can you remind me?
5 I can't decide _____ or not to do a course on memory training.
6 I've seen a website about _____ you can improve your memory. It's got some good ideas.

B Write the words in brackets in the correct order to make sentences.

1 (ask/don't know/I/to/who) ___*I don't know who to ask.*___
2 (rains/it/if/don't care/I) _____
3 (was/didn't realise/the time/he/what) _____
4 (drive/to/she/me/teach/'s going to/how) _____
5 (we/where/going/couldn't see/were/we) _____
6 (knows/keep/to/never/he/when/quiet) _____

C Complete the sentences for you.

1 I'm going to learn how _____
2 I sometimes can't remember what _____
3 I don't care whether _____
4 I can't decide where _____

Test 4 (Units 31–40)

A Circle the correct answer.

1 I was **going to/about to** practise the piano this evening but I forgot.

2 I wish I **don't have to/didn't have to** work for a living.

3 After we **will decorate/have decorated** the flat, we'll move in.

4 I don't know where he is. He **might be playing/might play** golf.

5 We're going to a concert tonight and another **one/the one** tomorrow.

6 Do you know a restaurant **whose/where** you can eat well?

7 I'll see you on Tuesday, **which/when** I get a day off.

8 The car looked a lot newer after it **had been cleaned/was being cleaned**.

9 He said he would come but he **hasn't/doesn't**.

10 I wonder whether **will they/they will** get married.

`10`

B Write the verbs in the correct form.

1 I was planning .... (retire) at 50 but I changed my mind.

2 I wish someone .... (answer) that telephone.

3 Tina wishes she .... (have) a new coat.

4 When you .... (read) that book can you take it back to the library?

5 While you .... (have) dinner, I'll pack the suitcases.

6 Her light's on. She must .... (study) in her room.

7 I couldn't use my car. It .... (service) at the garage.

8 Her cat was very hungry. It .... (not/feed) for two days.

9 I've forgotten what times the buses .... (run).

10 I've seen a good book about how .... (cook) spaghetti.

`10`

C Complete the sentences using the word in brackets and one other word.

1 A lot of people were .... lose their jobs. (due)

2 I don't like these apples. I prefer the .... over there. (other)

3 I love Paris. We stayed in a hotel .... year. (last)

4 I'm new here. I don't know .... go. (where)

5 I don't care .... has passed her driving test or not. She's still a good driver. (she)

`5`

D Complete the gaps with one word.

1 He can't _____ having lunch. I saw him in the office only a minute ago.

2 I wish I _____ swim but I can't.

3 What's the name of the person _____ car was stolen?

4 That's the hotel _____ we stayed last year.

5 It was after 7 o'clock at night, _____ is a bad time to go out shopping.

6 A decision had _____ made to offer everyone a pay increase.

7 'Let's go for a picnic.' '_____'s a good idea!'

8 When I first met _____ , Mary was working for a bank.

9 He doesn't know _____ or not to go out tonight.

10 I don't understand _____ the television isn't working. It's a mystery!

10

E Change two sentences into one. Use the word in brackets.

1 I won't buy the bag. I'll speak to my boyfriend first. (until)

....

2 Brush your teeth. Then please go to bed. (once)

....

3 My Uncle George is a doctor. He came to see me last night. (who)

....

4 My new jumper has shrunk. I spent a lot of money on it. (which)

....

5 Jan is studying medicine. Her mother's a doctor. (whose)

....

5

F Correct the mistakes.

1 What were you thinking <u>to do</u> tonight? ....

2 If only I <u>would be</u> taller. ....

3 Our house is <u>a one</u> on the left. ....

4 I can't decide <u>what do</u> tonight. ....

5 The money <u>was offered me</u> in an envelope. ....

6 He has good ideas but he never remembers <u>the good ideas</u>. ....

7 When <u>I've seen</u> you, I'll give you a present. ....

8 It <u>must be</u> raining – the roads are dry. ....

9 This is Jane, <u>that</u> is my best friend. ....

10 Tom <u>was always wanted</u> to be a footballer. ....

10

TOTAL

50

Verb forms

Present simple

Positive		Negative	
I/You/We/They	speak English.	I/You/We/They	don't (do not) speak Japanese.
He/She	speaks English.	He/She	doesn't (does not) speak Japanese.

Questions			Short answers					
Do	I/you/ we/they	speak English?	Yes,	I/you/ we/they	do.	No,	I/you/ we/they	don't.
Does	he/she			he/she	does.		he/she	doesn't.

Present continuous

Positive		Negative	
I'm (am)		I'm not (am not)	
He/She's (is)	waiting.	He/She isn't (is not)	waiting.
You/We/They're (are)		You/We/They aren't (are not)	

Questions			Short answers					
Am	I	leaving?	Yes,	I	am.	No,	I'm not.	
Is	he/she			he/she	is.		he/she isn't.	
Are	you/we/they			you/we/they	are.		you/we/they aren't.	

Past simple

Positive		Negative		
I/He/She/	walked. (regular)	I/He/She/	didn't	walk.
You/We/They	drove. (irregular)	You/We/They		drive.

Questions			Short answers		
Did	I/he/she/ you/we/they	go by bus?	Yes,	I/he/she/ you/we/they	did.
			No,		didn't.

Past continuous

Positive			Negative		
I/He/She	was	studying.	I/He/She	wasn't (was not)	studying.
You/We/They	were		You/We/They	weren't (were not)	

Questions			Short answers				
Was	I/he/she	studying?	Yes,	I/he/she	was.	No,	I/he/she wasn't.
Were	you/we/they			you/we/they	were.		we/you/they weren't.

Present perfect

Positive			Negative		
I/You've We/They've (have)		moved.	I/You/ We/They	haven't (have not)	moved.
He/She's (has)			He/She	hasn't (has not)	

Questions			Short answers						
Have	I/you/we/they	moved?	Yes,	I/you/we/they	have.	No,	I/you/we/they	haven't.
Has	he/she			he/she	has.		he/she	hasn't.

Present perfect continuous

Positive			Negative		
I/You've We/They've (have)		been swimming.	I/You/ We/They	haven't (have not)	been swimming.
He/She's (has)			He/She	hasn't (has not)	

Questions			Short answers						
Have	I/you/we/they	been swimming?	Yes,	I/you/we/they	have.	No,	I/you/we/they	haven't.
Has	he/she			he/she	has.		he/she	hasn't.

Past perfect

Positive			Negative		
I/You'd He/She'd (had) We/They'd		arrived.	I/You He/She We/They	hadn't (had not)	arrived.

Questions			Short answers					
Had	I/you/he/she we/they	arrived?	Yes,	I/you/he/she we/they	had.	No,	I/you/he/she we/they	hadn't.

Past perfect continuous

Positive			Negative		
I/You'd He/She'd (had) We/They'd		been working.	I/You He/She We/They	hadn't (had not)	been working.

Questions			Short answers					
Had	I/you/he/she we/they	been working?	Yes,	I you/he/she we/they	had.	No,	I/he/she we/they	hadn't.

Irregular verbs

VERB	PAST SIMPLE	PAST PARTICIPLE
be	was/were	been
beat	beat	beaten
become	became	become
begin	began	begun
bend	bent	bent
bet	bet	bet
bite	bit	bitten
blow	blew	blown
break	broke	broken
bring	brought	brought
build	built	built
burn	burned/burnt	burned/burnt
burst	burst	burst
buy	bought	bought
catch	caught	caught
choose	chose	chosen
come	came	come
cost	cost	cost
cut	cut	cut
deal	dealt	dealt
dig	dug	dug
do	did	done
draw	drew	drawn
dream	dreamed/dreamt	dreamed/dreamt
drink	drank	drunk
drive	drove	driven
eat	ate	eaten
fall	fell	fallen
feed	fed	fed
feel	felt	felt
find	found	found
fly	flew	flown
forget	forgot	forgotten
freeze	froze	frozen
get	got	got

VERB	PAST SIMPLE	PAST PARTICIPLE
give	gave	given
go	went	gone/been
grow	grew	grown
hang	hung/hanged	hung/hanged
have	had	had
hear	heard	heard
hide	hid	hidden
hit	hit	hit
hold	held	held
hurt	hurt	hurt
keep	kept	kept
kneel	kneeled/knelt	kneeled/knelt
know	knew	known
lay	laid	laid
lead	led	led
learn	learned/learnt	learned/learnt
leave	left	left
lend	lent	lent
let	let	let
lie	lay	lain
light	lit	lit
lose	lost	lost
make	made	made
mean	meant	meant
meet	met	met
pay	paid	paid
put	put	put
read	read	read
ride	rode	ridden
ring	rang	rung
rise	rose	risen
run	ran	run
say	said	said
see	saw	seen
sell	sold	sold
send	sent	sent
set up	set up	set up

VERB	PAST SIMPLE	PAST PARTICIPLE
shake	shook	shaken
shine	shone	shone
shoot	shot	shot
show	showed	shown
shrink	shrank	shrunk
shut	shut	shut
sing	sang	sung
sink	sank	sunk
sit	sat	sat
sleep	slept	slept
slide	slid	slid
smell	smelled/smelt	smelled/smelt
speak	spoke	spoken
spell	spelled/spelt	spelled/spelt
spend	spent	spent
spill	spilled/spilt	spilled/spilt
split	split	split
spoil	spoiled/spoilt	spoiled/spoilt
spread	spread	spread
stand	stood	stood
steal	stole	stolen
stick	stuck	stuck
swear	swore	sworn
swell	swelled	swelled/swollen
swim	swam	swum
take	took	taken
teach	taught	taught
tear	tore	torn
tell	told	told
think	thought	thought
throw	threw	thrown
understand	understood	understood
wake	woke	woken
wear	wore	worn
win	won	won
write	wrote	written

Spelling

Verb +*ing*

verb ends in *e*:	*e* +*ing*	verb ends in *ie*:	*ie* +*ying*
invite	→ inviting	lie →	lying
verb ends in 1 vowel + 1 consonant (stressed last syllable)		verb ends in *c*:	+*king*
run →	running	panic →	panicking
pre'fer →	pre'ferring		

Verb +*ed*

verb +*ed*	start	→	started
verb ends in *e:* +*d*	live	→	lived
	lie	→	lied
verb ends in consonant + *y: y* +*ied*	try	→	tried
verb ends in vowel + *y*	enjoy	→	enjoyed
BUT: *ay* → *aid*	pay	→	paid
	lay	→	laid
verb ends in 1 vowel + 1 consonant (stressed last syllable)	stop	→	stopped
	pre'fer		pre'ferred

Word +*s*, +*es*, +*ies*

word ends -*ch*/-*sh*/-*ss*/-*x*/-*z*/-*zz*/-*o:* +*es*		word ends in consonant +*y:* *y* +*ies*	
rush	→ rushes	try →	tries
watch	→ watches	baby →	babies
go	→ goes	word ends in -*f*/*fe*:	*f(e)* +*ves*
potato	→ potatoes	shelf →	shelves
BUT abbreviations		knife →	knives
photo	→ photos	BUT	
piano	→ pianos	chief →	chiefs

Adjective +*er*, +*est*

one-syllable adjective, ends in 1 vowel + 1 consonant			
hot	→ hotter, hottest	big →	bigger, biggest
two-syllable adjective, ends in -*y: y* +*ier* –*iest*			
easy	→ easier, easiest	tidy →	tidier, tidiest

ⓘvowels: a e i o u; consonants: b c d f g h j k l m n p q r s t v w x y z
one-syllable words: work, start, big
two-syllable words: travel (trav+el), begin (be+gin), pretty (pre+tty)

State verbs & verb patterns

Common state verbs

Existence: I am a chef. be, exist	Measurements: It costs a lot of money. contain, consist of, cost, weigh
Perception/senses: She seems nice. appear (= seem), feel, hear, look, notice, realise, recognise, see, seem, smell, sound, taste	Emotions: He loves coffee. admire, (not) care, dislike, forgive, hate, hope (to), like, love, prefer, regret, refuse (to), want (to), wish (to)
Mental states: I agree with you. agree, believe, doubt, expect, feel (= think), forget, imagine, know, mean, mind, realise, remember, suppose, think (=believe), understand, wonder	Possession: This coat belongs to my father. belong, have, have got, own, possess

Verb patterns

+ *-ing*: He finished reading.

admit, adore, appreciate, avoid, can't face, can't help, can't stand, carry on, consider, delay, deny, detest, discuss, dislike, enjoy, fancy, feel like, finish, give up, imagine, involve, keep (= continue), mention, mind, miss, postpone, practise, put off, resent, resist, risk, suggest, understand

verb + *to*-infinitive: I expect to see her.

afford, agree, appear, arrange, ask, attempt, can't afford, can't wait, choose, claim, decide, demand, deserve, expect, fail, grow, happen, help, hope, intend, learn, manage, mean, need, neglect, offer, pay, plan, prefer, prepare, pretend, promise, refuse, request, seem, tend, threaten, turn out, wait, want, wish, would like/love/hate

verb + bare infinitive: I might go.

'd better, 'd rather, let, make (but in the passive: I was made to…), modals (may, might, can, should etc but ought to)

Answer key

Unit 1

A 2 What sort of music does Tom like?
3 Will you get more money in the new job? 4 Which countries would you like to visit? 5 Who did you meet last night? 6 Doesn't she live in New York? 7 How many people came to your party? 8 Whose car did you borrow to get to work?

B 2 What do you usually do in the evenings? (Answers will vary.) 3 Where did you go on your holidays last year? 4 What's your favourite colour? 5 Who gets up first in your house? 6 How many cups of coffee have you had this week? 7 How often do you go out for dinner? 8 How much excercise do you do each week?

C 2 Which towns will/do you visit on the way? – e 3 Which tour costs less? – c 4 What can you see in Oxford? – i 5 Where does the coach stop? – b 6 Who lives in the castle? – h 7 Don't children get a reduction? – g 8 Whose wallet is this? – a 9 How soon will/does the coach leave? – d

Unit 2

A 2 I quite often bite my nails. 3 I get a headache every so often. 4 I work very late about three times a week. 5 Now and then my mouth feels dry. 6 I get angry several times a day. 7 I am late for appointments again and again.

B Answers will vary.

Unit 3

A 2 of 3 for 4 from 5 with 6 about 7 from

B 2 is the letter from 3 is she smiling about (for) 4 is she waiting for 5 is she looking at 6 is she reading about

Unit 4

A 2 're always arguing 3 is always going off 4 's always losing 5 's always giving 6 's always complaining

B 2 do you think; 'm enjoying 3 is becoming; remember 4 Do you like; 'm thinking 5 are getting; know; are always telling me

C 2 is only going up 3 think 4 have 5 is starting 6 like 7 'm always getting on 8 is improving 9 don't feel 10 'm seeing

Unit 5

A 2 while 3 for 4 during 5 during 6 by

B 2 during 3 while 4 until 5 By 6 until 7 while 8 for 9 by 10 while

Unit 6

A 3 would never stop 4 would leave 5 x 6 would usually go 7 x 8 would play 9 x 10 x

B [Answers will vary] 2 I used to live … 3 I didn't use to be … 4 … but I used to when … 5 … I would often …

Unit 7

A 2 Every 3 All 4 the whole 5 Each 6 Every 7 all of your

B 2 each 3 whole 4 all 5 whole 6 every

Unit 8

A 2 went 3 seeing 4 starting 5 finding 6 could

B 2 Before leading/she led an army against the British, Joan of Arc worked on her father's farm. 3 Three years after agreeing/he agreed an arms treaty with the US, Mikhail Gorbachev was awarded the Nobel Peace Prize. 4 Before ending/she ended her life, Cleopatra asked to be buried with the Roman Marc Antony.

Unit 9

A 2 quite 3 a bit 4 rather an 5 quite a
6 a rather

B 2 fairly cheap 3 rather busy 4 a really old
5 quite an interesting

Unit 10

A 3 had seen 4 had paid 5 hadn't heard
6 had had 7 hadn't had 8 had started
9 hadn't booked

B 2 d 3 g 4 f 5 a 6 c 7 b 8 e

C 2 had already studied 3 had already
started 4 had already changed 5 had
already made 6 had already had 7 had
recorded 8 hadn't lived

D 2 had she already changed; No, she hadn't.
3 Had she already made; Yes, she had.
4 Had she already had; No she hadn't.
5 had she recorded; 21 6 had she lived; 34

Test 1 (Units 1–10)

A 1 will the meeting 2 phones her friends
every few minutes 3 did you go out with
last night 4 is always breaking 5 until
6 used to be 7 every 8 playing 9 fairly
10 had closed

B 1 Where does she work? 2 Where did
you get the book (from)? 3 Shouldn't
you be more careful? 4 Who invited you
to the party? 5 Where does the plane
leave from? 6 Had you already paid for
the tickets? 7 Whose car was stolen last
night? 8 What was the book about? 9
How long have you been living here
(there)?
10 Who told you the news?

C 1 I visit my father most afternoons./ Most
afternoons I visit my father. 2 She rarely
reads a newspaper. 3 We all get lost from
time to time./From time to time we all get
lost. 4 He hardly ever cooks for himself.
5 We have to work late twice a week.
/Twice a week we have to work late.

D 1 was having 2 had already left 3 is
always getting 4 'm thinking 5 usually
prefer 6 going / I go 7 had never been
8 Are you enjoying 9 is getting 10 went

E 1 … I would go for … 2 … used to
have … 3 Did you use to live … 4 They
would meet … 5 I didn't use to have …

F 1 All 2 quite 3 whole 4 Each 5 rather

G 1 rang 2 for 3 a whole month 4 quite a
lot 5 by/before

Unit 11

A 2 haven't seen; went; met; wasn't 3 left; still
hasn't arrived 4 has been playing (has
played); first took up; bought 5 did you
speak 6 has already started. Haven't you got

B Answers will vary.

Unit 12

A 2 He shouldn't eat 3 If I were you, I'd
buy him 4 He'd better not watch 5 He
ought to go

B 2 shouldn't go 3 ought to wear 4 'd
better carry 5 I were you, I'd leave
6 'd better not climb

Unit 13

A 2 to turn 3 not putting
4 could possibly shut 5 would mind
looking after

B 2 if you'd mind doing me a favour/if you
could do me a favour 3 you could not
make so much noise/you could make less
noise 4 give me a lift into town 5 you
could lend me some money, could you
6 not dropping litter in the street

Unit 14

A 2 as soon as 3 while 4 after 5 before
6 as soon as

B 2 As soon as the post arrives can you give
me a ring? 3 Don't use my computer
while I'm out! 4 Tell the kids to go to
bed as soon as the film finishes. 5 Don't
forget to clean up the flat after your
friends leave. 6 Can you wash the dishes
before you go to work in the morning?

Unit 15

A 2 one another 3 on your own 4 your own 5 yourselves 6 itself 7 each other's

B 2 themselves 3 my own 4 each other (one another) 5 ourselves 6 myself

Unit 16

A 2 in case 3 in order to 4 for 5 so that 6 so as not to; to

B 2 so that 3 order to 4 in case 5 for

C 2 as to stop (that we can stop) 3 order to complain 4 in case we damage/so that we don't damage 5 to achieve/in order to achieve/so as to achieve/so that we achieve 6 so that we protect 7 finding out

D Answers will vary.

Unit 17

A 2 e 3 b 4 a 5 d

B 2 to be a pilot 3 if you took a taxi 4 take any 5 went swimming 6 had gone to Paris

Unit 18

A 1b to watch 2a to meet; b seeing 3a to buy; b looking 4a showing; b to have 5a talking; b to meet 6a leaving; b to phone 7a park; b playing

B 2 touch 3 drop 4 burning 5 queuing

C 2 suffering 3 to go 4 to exchange 5 moving 6 to stop

D Answers will vary.

Unit 19

A 2 It had been raining 3 I had been crying 4 Had you been waiting; hadn't 5 I had been sleeping

B 2 had phoned 3 had been working 4 had been looking forward to 5 had only been trying 6 had forgotten 7 had already been

Unit 20

A 2 need to be 3 need to organise 4 needn't wear/don't need to wear 5 need to ask 6 needn't eat/don't need to eat

B 2 didn't need to spend 3 needn't have been worried 4 didn't need to take 5 needn't have given them

Test 2 (Units 11–20)

A 1 haven't seen 2 ought to go 3 could possibly give 4 finish 5 by herself 6 in case 7 it if you phoned 8 to interrupt 9 'd been working 10 didn't need to catch

B 1 went; haven't been 2 have you been decorating 3 were; 'd look for 4 leave; should go 5 to eat; (to) go 6 lending 7 sneezing 8 had been working 9 had cooked 10 don't need

C 1 Not 2 while 3 before 4 so 5 to 6 each 7 by 8 on 9 yourself 10 one

D 1 taking 2 cooking 3 to get 4 spending 5 to say

E 1 You'd better not stay up too late. 2 She ought to buy some new clothes. 3 Do you think you could (possibly) turn off the light? 4 Would you mind not driving so fast? 5 I was wondering if you could call a taxi. 6 I won't go out in case he calls. 7 We'd rather stay at home. 8 I'd prefer it if you left now. 9 We don't need to stand. 10 Try to be calm.

F 1 wrote 2 to learn 3 to water 4 had eaten 5 needn't

Unit 21

A 2 unless 3 if 4 if 5 if; unless 6 Even if 7 if 8 When

B 2 Be; know 3 's; is always 4 shake/can shake/should shake; don't grip 5 call; 's

C Answers will vary.

D 2 can't travel; you have 3 had more time 4 'll be there; isn't delayed 5 could get 6 were; 'd go 7 stay

Unit 22

A 2 be 3 spend 4 eating 5 working 6 swim

B Answers will vary. 2 ... get used to people taking your photograph all the time. 3 ... get used to not going to work every day. 4 ... get used to looking after yourself. 5 ... get used to waking up during the night.

C 2 be/get used to speaking 3 get used to driving 4 used to be 5 'm used to working 6 'm not used to eating 7 'm used to 8 'm getting used to it

Unit 23

A 2 are due to 3 is about to 4 is (are) likely to 5 is due to 6 is to

B 2 'm going to get 3 'm taking 4 'll get 5 'll be 6 doesn't start 7 's going to be

C 2 're meeting 3 's going to be 4 'll have 5 'm taking/'m going to take 6 does it start 7 might be 8 's not due to finish 9 's flying 10 's about the leave 11 are likely to be/will be 12 'll see

D Answers will vary. 2 I'll answer it/I'll get it. 3 What time does the last train leave? 4 I'm going to buy my father a wallet (for his birthday). 5 He is to meet the Queen on his last day. 6 I'm having a haircut next Tuesday. 7 It's going to snow soon. 8 Manchester United are going to win. 9 There will be more pollution in the world.

Unit 24

A 2 as much 3 so few 4 far more 5 much more 6 as many

B 2 many 3 fewer 4 much 5 less 6 as much 7 as many 8 much

Unit 25

A 2 Who else 3 anywhere else 4 No-one else/Nobody else 5 What else 6 Where else 7 someone else's 8 anything else

B 2 Someone else 3 What else 4 everywhere else 5 How else 6 nothing else 7 anyone else

Unit 26

A 2 do 3 made 4 doing 5 make 6 do; do 7 done; make

B Answers will vary.

Unit 27

A 2 expected me to take part in 3 didn't like me missing 4 involved me/us discussing 5 stopped me playing 6 didn't mind me taking 7 warned me not to train

B 2 Ivan getting up 3 me ages to find 4 him to buy 5 prevent him going 6 a lot of time trying

Unit 28

A 2 as 3 As; like 4 as 5 like; like 6 As 7 as; like; as 8 Like

B 2 As I was worried, I couldn't sleep. (I couldn't sleep as I was worried.) 3 I woke up early, as I knew I would. 4 As we were getting up, we heard a noise. (We heard a noise as we were getting up.) 5 They found us, as I said they would.

C 2 as if 3 like 4 like 5 as 6 like 7 as if; were 8 As

D 2 ... smells like Indian food. 3 ... tastes as if/as though/like it's made of cardboard. 4 ... sounds like thunder. 5 ... looks as if/as though/like a bomb's hit it.

E 2 As 3 like 4 like 5 as if 6 as if 7 as 8 as 9 like

Unit 29

A 2 so 3 so 4 not 5 so 6 so 7 not 8 not

B 2 I guess so 3 I hope so 4 I'm afraid not
5 I don't imagine so/I imagine not 6 I
guess not 7 told you so

Unit 30

A 2 the next day 3 the day before 4 going
5 that day 6 that 7 had 8 would 9 had
to 10 might

B 2 'How well can you cook?' 3 'I've been
trained as a top chef.' 4 'Can/Could you
give me some ideas for a meal?' 5 'Don't
worry. We'll think of something.'

C 2 said; was 3 me; I had 4 I would 5 to
phone; needed

D 2 he was sorry he couldn't/can't get here
today; if he could see you another day
3 he would phone back later 4 if you
would want to see her medical records
5 what would be the best time to see you
next week 6 me to phone her as soon as
you got in this morning

E 1 ... me how many cups of coffee I
drank/drink a day; ... her that I have/
had ...; ... (that) that was too much
coffee; ... me to try to drink more water.
2 ... what I'd had for lunch the previous
week; ... I had eaten meat every day; ...
if I had eaten any green vegetables; ...her
I had had a salad one day.

Test 3 (Units 21–30)

A 1 don't bring 2 used to 3 due to 4 far
5 anything else 6 done 7 to step 8 As
9 suppose so 10 had spoken

B 1 score 2 won't get; call 3 were/was;
would marry 4 working 5 living 6 'm
playing (going to play)
7 'll be 8 to stay 9 criticising
10 would like

C 1 fewer 2 so 3 else 4 not 5 so

D 1 Tickets/The tickets are likely to be
expensive. 2 The film's about to start.
3 ...me to take off... 4 ...me
travelling... 5 ...taking...

E 1 nearly as much 2 so little 3 Nobody
else 4 make 5 like

F 1 ... had mended the door. 2 ... if I
liked their flat. 3 ... what she was doing
the next day. 4 ... had to come and see
him. 5 ... not to move that picture.

G 1 didn't have 2 living 3 's going to be
4 What else would you like? 5 do 6 cry
7 you going 8 as if/like 9 like 10 know

Unit 31

A 2 thinking of buying 3 about to
4 due to 5 going to 6 planning to

B 1 due to arrive 2 planning to put;
thinking of going

Unit 32

A 2 was 3 could 4 had; could 5 were
6 could meet

B Answers will vary. 2 was/were...
3 was/were ... 4 could ... 5 could ...

C 2 the press would leave him 3 more
people would try 4 the newspapers
didn't invent/wouldn't invent 5 she
could lead 6 he didn't have to spend
7 he was/were watching

D 2 ... he would help/helped with the
cleaning. 3 ... I had more time to read a
book. 4 ... I didn't get a headache in the
evenings. 5 ... I didn't have to go to
work tomorrow.

Unit 33

A 2 you've looked 3 I'm making 4 I've paid 5 we get 6 we've checked 7 we're sitting

B 2 I'll wait here until you get/'ve got… 3 Once the taxi's arrived/arrives, we must leave… 4 As soon as we've seen Keiko, we'll find … 5 By the time we get/'ve got back at 10.00, it'll be …

Unit 34

A 1 be having 2 be rehearsing; be playing 3 be getting

B 1 may/might be getting 2 can't be working; may/might be visiting 3 must be watching; may/might be doing 4 may/might not be telling; can't be doing

Unit 35

A 2 a 3 d 4 b 5 c

B 2 The one 3 Another one; one 4 Ones 5 the ones 6 the other ones 7 another one

Unit 36

A 2 when 3 whose 4 where 5 where 6 when

B 2 where they do the job 3 an Asian country whose economy is growing 4 the day when we have to make 5 a restaurant where we can get

Unit 37

A 2 when 3 which 4 who 5 where 6 whose 7 which 8 where

B 2 Thailand, which used to be known as Siam, changed its name in 1939. 3 The King, who is called 'The Great' by his people, has ruled since 1946. 4 July, when the rainy season begins, can be quite uncomfortable. 5 The best time to go is February, which is when the weather is at its best. (February, when the weather is at its best, is the best time to go.) 6 Chiang Mai, where you can buy beautiful handicrafts, is in the north of the country.

C 2 Unfortunately, he's married to Karen, who I don't like very much. 3 We flew from Switzerland, where we were staying for the summer. 4 Melbourne, where my friend has a house, is the cultural capital of Australia. 5 Tara, whose daughter has just moved to Australia, came with us. 6 Spring, when there are flowers everywhere, is the best time to go. (Spring is the best time to go, when there are flowers everywhere.)

D Answers will vary.

Unit 38

A 2 had been destroyed 3 were being comforted 4 had been stolen 5 were being educated 6 was being questioned

B 2 will be shown to the foreign visitors 3 were told a lot of lies 4 were being brought a new agreement to sign 5 had been offered to the finance director

C 2 made 3 was (is) 4 were (are) not being allowed 5 was (is) being used 6 hadn't (hasn't) been fed

D 2 was being watched 3 were eating 4 was broken down 5 rushed in 6 tied us up 7 were taken 8 wanted 9 had been kidnapped 10 weren't allowed 11 didn't know 12 had been asked 13 had refused 14 were rescued

Unit 39

A 2 Othello 3 Desdemona 4 Othello 5 in the theatre 6 the production at the Apollo Theatre 7 the actors 8 on stage 9 very good 10 the teenage audience 11 the play/the production 12 loved it

B 2 them 3 it 4 there; then 5 that; did 6 do; not

C 1 that 2 they did 3 Their; ones 4 they; That 5 then

D 2 their red trousers; looked incredible 3 she went to California; tried to get a job in the movies 4 his strange accent; could understand Rory 5 he left the company; never saw John again

Unit 40

A 2 what 3 if/whether 4 what 5 whether
6 how

B 2 I don't care if it rains. 3 He didn't
realise what the time was. 4 She's going
to teach me how to drive. 5 We couldn't
see where we were going. 6 He never
knows when to keep quiet.

C Answers will vary.

Test 4 (Units 31-40)

A 1 going to 2 didn't have to 3 have
decorated 4 might be playing 5 one
6 where 7 when 8 had been cleaned
9 hasn't 10 they will

B 1 to retire 2 would answer 3 had/could
have 4 've read 5 're having 6 be
studying 7 was being serviced 8 hadn't
been fed 9 run 10 to cook

C 1 due to 2 other ones 3 there last
4 where to 5 whether/if she

D 1 be 2 could 3 whose 4 where 5 which
6 been 7 That 8 her 9 whether 10 why

E I won't buy the bag until I speak/'ve
spoken to my boyfriend. 2 Once you've
brushed your teeth, please go to bed.
3 My Uncle George, who came to see
me last night, is a doctor. 4 My new
jumper, which I spent a lot of money on,
has shrunk. 5 Jan, whose mother's a
doctor, is studying medicine.

F 1 of doing 2 were 3 the one 4 what to
do 5 was offered to me 6 them 7 I see
8 can't be 9 who 10 always wanted

Acknowledgements

I would particularly like to thank Alison Sharpe for her help, guidance and support during the editing of this series. My thanks also to Jessica Roberts for her expert editing of the material and to Kamae Design and Nick Schon for their excellent design and artwork.

The publisher would like to thank the following for permission to reproduce photographs.

AKG-Images, London pp. 72 (Vermeer, Woman in blue reading a letter, Rijksmuseum, Amsterdam), 75 (Frederic Bazille, La Robe Rose/ Photo Erich Lessing); Alamy pp. 14 (John Bower), 35 (Gabi Wojciech), 38 (Janine Wiedel); The Bridgeman Art Library p. 73 (Leonardo da Vinci, Mona Lisa, Louvre, Paris/Giraudon); Courtesy of Continuum Books p. 11; Corbis pp. 71 (Auguste Rodin, The Thinker /Bettmann), 74 (Edward Hopper, Automat /Francis G. Mayer), 76 (Pierre Auguste Renoir, Leontine Reading/ Christie's Images), 9, 51 (David Beckham/Dan Chung), 51 (J Lo/Ning Chiu/Entertainment Pictures), 51 (Renee Zellweger/Tama Herrick), 61 (© S.I.N./Melanie Cox); Getty Images pp. 16 (Hulton Archive), 51 (Julia Roberts/Evan Agostini), 51 (Antonio Banderas/Sean Gallup), 51 (Elton John/Robert Mora), 56 (Pornchai Kittiwongsakul); The Kobal Collection p. 28; Nature Picture Library p. 24 (Miles Barton); Still Pictures p. 43 (Jorgen Schytte)

Every effort has been made to reach the copyright holders; the publishers would be pleased to hear from anyone whose rights they have unknowingly infringed.

Produced by Kamae Design, Oxford.
Illustrations by Nick Schon

Grammar in Practice

	SBN-10	SBN-13
Level 1 Beginner	0521 665760	978 0521 665766
Level 2 Elementary	0521 665663	978 0521 665667
Level 3 Pre-intermediate	0521 540410	978 0521 540414
Level 4 Intermediate	0521 540429	978 0521 540421
Level 5 Intermediate to upper-intermediate	0521 618282	978 0521 618281
Level 6 Upper-intermediate	0521 618290	978 0521 618298

Vocabulary in Practice

	SBN-10	SBN-13
Level 1 Beginner	0521 010802	978 0521 010801
Level 2 Elementary	0521 010829	978 0521 010825
Level 3 Pre-intermediate	0521 753759	978 0521 753753
Level 4 Intermediate	0521 753767	978 0521 753760
Level 5 Intermediate to upper-intermediate	0521 601258	978 0521 601252
Level 6 Upper-intermediate	0521 601266	978 0521 601269